7 KEYS 2 SUCCESS:

UNLOCKING THE PASSION
FOR DIVERSITY

Rosalyn Taylor O'Neale

Llumina Press

ISBN: 1-59526-092-7

Printed in the United States of America by Llumina Press

Table of Contents

Chapter Ten - Closure

Acknowledgments

Over the years I have been blessed with wonderful friends and colleagues. My words and success have been shaped by those who have always taken time to talk and listen. I thank the following people for being my friends, and influencing my thinking – Ross Brown, Fiona Devan, Edie Fraser, Tom Freston, JoAnne Griffith, Robert Hayles, Bill Meade, Tim Solso and Barbara Walker. The MTV Networks Executive Diversity Leaders Class of 2004 – Tom Ascheim, Tony Dunaif, Jason Hirschhorn, Pam Kaufman, Peter Low, Chris Parr, Alicin Reidy and Marva Smalls – taught me much more than I taught them. Maxine Fassberg, Joi Gordon, Flo Kennedy and Don Zimmerman influenced my sense of what's important.

I am also grateful to the people whose expertise made 7 Keys a reality: Bucky Fox – the editor who took my words and arranged them for reading, Michelle DeFillippo – the designer who understood my vision and put it on the jacket and the wonderful people at Llumina Press who gathered, harvested, and produced this book.

I could never have done this without the humor, intelligence, and spirit of my business partner, Sheila. For thirteen years she has been the Barnes of Barnes, O'Neale & Assoc., but more importantly for 26 years she has been my best friend.

I want to thank my honey, Mendy, for putting up with my writing insanity. On the days when I spent hours sitting at my computer trying to figure out if I should use a semicolon or a comma, I knew I could always count on her love and support. Thank you both for taking care of me all the years that led up to this work.

Lastly, I want to thank my mom for teaching me to be irreverent and funny – although she is gone, her voice resonates throughout the book –and I am deeply grateful to God for all the rest.

Preface

For years people have said, "You should write a book." I took their words to heart and sat down to write. I'm disciplined, so I wrote from seven in the morning until late at night. My laptop and me - at my desk, on the couch, at the park and on the bluffs. Everything I knew about diversity poured out of me onto the computer screen. The plan was to write, write, write, and then go back and edit. One Wednesday when I felt satisfied I'd captured every brilliant insight into the subject, I realized I had written a paltry twenty-one pages! Twenty-one pages! That's a pamphlet, not a book. Panic set in! I found a Web site that told me how many computer-generated pages translated into book pages; now I had thirty-two pages. Not a book, but a fat pamphlet. So here's my fat pamphlet.

In the beginning I wrote this book so I would become famous. I knew that after reading the first chapter Dr. Phil would call and ask if I would join him to discuss the impact of diversity on teenagers. This would be followed by a call from Oprah, who would ask me to help her change an entire town from a racist or homophobic mess into a warm, loving, open and welcoming village – the epitome of goodness.

This vision was followed by an equally silly fantasy: I was writing a book with *all of the answers* to all of the dilemmas the journey toward inclusion will bring to you and your organization. I envisioned that contained in this fat pamphlet would be every answer to every question out there and that every answer would be complete, quirky and amazing – but as the Executive Diversity Leader class of 2004 reminded me, "There are no answers, only interesting dialogues" (my words, which I'm chewing slowly for better digestion).

So I decided to write something simple and readable, with ideas you can recall like the words to a song or a nursery rhyme. I wanted to write a book that didn't have a lot of pages (ergo the fat pamphlet), more than the *Five Minute Manager* and fewer than the latest book about Donald Trump.

I chose to write about my work and not my life because I'm known more for what I do than who I am, although the two aren't really that separate. However, it might help to know a few important things about me. I was raised in the segregated South. I have pictures of me as a skinny ten-year-old standing below signs that say "coloreds only." I remember driving through Mississippi on our way to Louisiana knowing that at least once during the trip to visit my brother, we would be stopped (my mother was legally White and "high yella," my father a dark-skinned "Negro") and my father would have to carefully navigate racism. That was the daily certainty. It is also true that I come from a family that cared about others. My mother taught mentally retarded children in an inner city school after twenty years as a social worker. My father was a beat cop and finally a detective with the Louisville police department. My brother became a firefighter and today works with troubled youth. The experience of segregation, which is the extreme form of exclusion, and the requirement to care about others definitely influenced my choices. So did money. I received my master's degree in Social Work and realized that I could make more money (a lot more) caring about corporate executives than those in the social welfare system – so yes, I opted for the money and ultimately found the socially redeeming work of affirmative action, diversity and inclusion.

I have seen it all – the good and truly ugly sides of inclusion and exclusion. I've been privy to conversations that demonstrated the great heart and most despicable and dishonest behaviors of some of the most powerful men and women in business. I am still here because I've been involved with six or seven powerful individuals who committed to do whatever it took to make their workplace humane and benevolent. Those rare few are the reason I continue to lead and live this work. This book is for those who follow in their footsteps. It is written to honor the brave ones who drove their companies to become *better* before it was trendy and correct. It is for them that I present this simple and helpful notion: There are seven keys that lead to successful initiatives, hence the title *7 Keys 2 Success* ($^7K^2S$).

Most of us think of keys as the things that open doors and provide entry. Another definition appropriate for this conversation is that keys are "a) the aspect of something that, once understood, provides a full understanding or explanation of the whole and b) a place that is strategically vital in gaining access to or controlling a larger area."[i] I will do my best to give you ideas and tools that will give you access and insight into creating and maintaining a diverse and inclusive environment.

These seven keys open the door to *Success*. This is important because every organization I've ever worked with or consulted has the word "Success" written on its victory banner. Success is more elusive than profit, and often worth more to the ego. Managers and leaders want to *be* successful, to be *viewed as* successful and *surround themselves* with successful people. Employees are pleased when they can say they have a successful career or successfully completed a project. In the self-help/management section of one Barnes & Noble bookstore are 82 books with "Success" in the title.

But by themselves the seven keys are not enough, a dish but not a meal. The missing ingredient is passion. It's the difference between eating a dish prepared by someone who merely followed the recipe, and eating a meal cooked by someone with a love for food, a passion for the feast. The lover of food adds a pinch of salt the way her grandmother did, a sprig of mint – a tradition from her Southern heritage and olive oil she brought back from Israel. The person who adds love and passion will simply create a richer and tastier meal.

And so I write about ways to unlock and unleash an individual, group or organization's *Passion for Diversity.* Passion is more emotional than intellectual. It doesn't come as much from the mouth as it comes from the soul. When it appears, it is forceful, powerful and intense – not moderate or passive. A passion *for* diversity is a fiery and fervent emotional desire to be surrounded by and engaged with a variety of people and experiences. That **is** diversity.

This book is for individuals and organizations. The size, product, service, customer or age of the organization does not matter. If your company or group has 50,000 or 50 employees, there is one truth: As someone once said, "Organizations are a network of promises and commitments made between people." Chief executive officer (CEO), purchasing manager and administrative assistant are positions connected by a web of commitments and responsibilities to other titles in the company. The CEO, manager and assistant are also people, with unique individual histories, beliefs, talents and values. The *job title* that understands and embraces the seven keys will be a part of an energized and successful organization. The *person* with the passion for diversity will experience a fuller, more engaging life.

It is my commitment to go beyond simply extolling the virtues of diversity and inclusion (most who read books with "Diversity" in the title are already convinced of its merit) and to provide a road map that leaders and managers can use to develop and maintain an environment of healthy debate. I promise to provide a toolbox of techniques anyone can apply to improve his or her ability to confront and resolve difficult issues.

The majority of the experiences I describe in this book come from twenty-seven years of working closely with four large U.S.-based global companies. These organizations represent the consumer, technology, communications and manufacturing industries. I was initially going to do a large research project. Then I realized I have more than a quarter of a century of exploration of this topic. So although I have 61 books and over 150 articles covering every table and shelf in my office, what I've put on paper is mostly from my head and my heart.

I've changed the companies' and individuals' names to protect the innocent and the unaware. I've given the four major companies names to simplify the references. Any similarity to real companies is coincidental. All of the quotes come from real people, although only a few are identified by their real names. Some of the examples are a melding of two or three events that have a common theme or thread. Where I've taken license I've done so to add clarity.

Chapter one

first things first

Looking for Information About ...		Look Here First
About the Book – Who, What ...	⇨	Page 2
Definitions	⇨	Page 4
The Seven Keys	⇨	Page 11, 146
Four Major Business Case Rationales	⇨	Page 33
Recipe for a Business Case	⇨	Page 46
Characteristics of Leaders	⇨	Page 57
Six Negative Road Signs	⇨	Page 72
Tips for Leaders	⇨	Page 73
Executive Diversity and Inclusion Councils	⇨	Page 80
Developing Diversity Leaders	⇨	Page 83
Designing an Awareness Training Session	⇨	Page 92
Tools to Help Managers	⇨	Page 106
Using the 7Keys Scorecard®	⇨	Page 127

The Three Stages	$\Rightarrow$	Page 137
Answers to the Questions	$\Rightarrow$	Page 149

The 5 W's

WHO

This book is for:

- Those who are chartered with driving their organization's diversity and inclusion initiative; human resources, learning & development, community relations, supplier diversity and legal.
- CEOs who wish to increase the return on the dollars they are spending on their diversity and inclusion initiative.
- Leaders and managers in any size organization, producing any product or service anywhere.
- People who want their organization to *soar*!

WHAT

You will find:
A structured approach to diversity and inclusion initiatives.
Seven ideas that I know can take any organization from confusion to success – guaranteed!

WHEN

This guide is helpful at any stage of your organization's development.

- Use it to get started.
- Use it to determine where you are.
- Use it to plan for the next steps.
- Use it when the effort has slowed or stopped.
- Use it to maintain momentum.

WHERE

Any province, town or city in any country, on any continent. Some of you may be skeptical, but the ideas presented here have been successfully implemented in major companies in Europe, Asia, North & South America, Australia and Africa.

WHY

There are hundreds of books on diversity and inclusion. Many are written by academics who are intelligent but who may not be grounded in the challenges you face everyday. Often books are written by someone selling you something – it's the American way, but the questions and answers lead back to the product. This book is the result of a quarter of a century of work on the inside and the outside. I've struggled, been driven to distraction, had moments of elation and despair and continued on this journey. This one is written for you.

First Things First

Steven Covey's[ii] 3rd Habit is "Put First Things First." The most important "first" is that I have been blessed, lucky and watched over for 54 years. Everything in this book is tied to that fundamental truth. I'm more amazed than anyone else at my great fortune: doing work I love and I believe contributes to making this planet a better place.

I wrote the first iteration of the $^7K^2S$ in 1990, shortly after I left Digital Equipment Corporation (DEC), where I was the U.S. valuing differences manager. Over the next fourteen years while working for some of the largest and most complex global organizations, (American Express, Cummins Inc., Honeywell, Intel, Kaiser Permanente, Lawrence Livermore Laboratory) twelve years as an external consultant and two as the executive vice president, Diversity Initiatives, for MTV Networks, I have tested the Keys for their authenticity, validity and usefulness. I've modified them, but never abandoned a single one. I've added the notion of faith as number seven because in the final analysis you have to believe if you prepare and execute your plans; that *you* can do it, that *your organization* can do it and that it's worth the trouble.

The Keys are not epiphanies, thoughts worthy of stone etching, but rather straightforward processes that increase the likelihood you will be successful at creating diverse and inclusive organizations.

My goal is to ensure you understand what the seven elements are, how to use them, their relationship to one another – and most importantly you can see how they can be integrated into the daily life of the organization and can be applied to any venture.

Lastly, I sought to write a book that touches readers as often as it teaches. I want this book to provide guidance to pioneers and tourists as they set off on this journey. I hope you will find a story or a question that resonates with your experiences.

I have in my thirty-plus years of consulting and teaching been blessed to hear that my words have moved people. Some have even said my ideas "changed their lives." In these pages are two or three thoughts that I hope will touch you or maybe even cause the chain reaction that changes your life. You don't have to read every page. If you skim through and ask for guidance, I believe that what you're looking for, what's missing or important will appear.

Definitions

The language I use is specific. In this discipline words carry emotional as well as structural meaning. A person will say "there's no *diversity* in this organization," and the listener's understanding can be very different from the speaker's meaning of the word "diversity." Additionally, many terms, such as prejudice or privilege are loaded and carry significant baggage.

> **Diversity** – In an article in 1995 I stated, "I use 'differences' and 'diversity' interchangeably." I have since changed this. Today I define diversity as the characteristics we have in common (similarities) and those that are unlike others (differences) **and** *the impact* our differences and similarities have on our interactions – the impact that my being like you or different from you has on my ability to be comfortable with you, to trust you and to work with you.

> **Visible diversity** is used to describe characteristics that are easy to recognize when meeting someone. These include race, color, ethnicity, age, (some) disabilities and gender.

These characteristics are not dependent on the situation or conditions, e.g., the traditional garb of a Catholic priest at a monastery, or "in-group" knowledge such as a rainbow flag or pink triangle pin.

Inclusion is the "addition of something or someone to, or the presence of somebody or something in a group or mixture."[iii] In organizations it is creating the opportunity for many (or all) voices and perspectives to be heard. In this book it refers to practices that actively and passively encourage and allow individuals and groups to contribute, to have a say and to help direct the efforts of a team, group or organization.

Initiative describes the work that takes an organization from unconscious incompetence to unconscious competence[iv]. I used the word *initiative* defined as "a plan or strategy designed to deal with a particular problem [or challenge]."[v] I use this word alternately with the term *journey*.

Journey – Where you might normally expect to see the word *initiative* in this book, you may see *journey* as in "a gradual passing from one state to another regarded as more advanced, for example from innocence to mature awareness."[vi] A journey also connotes continuation rather than arrival or destination. Seeing this word where you expect to see *initiative* may be awkward at first, like reading the dialect in a Zora Neale Hurston novel, but I hope it'll become easy on the ears and eyes with a little practice.

Managing diversity is the processes and practices that incorporate the diversity - the parts - in the organization in ways that maximize their contribution to the whole, the organization.

Biases or mental models are the set of values, the background, experiences and cultural definitions that influence my view of people and the world. Think of them as an imaginary set of lenses that are implanted in my eyes at birth. Every experience colors my lens (i.e., my grandmother's dislike of Jewish people, the major news stories of my youth and the composition of my neighborhood). Consequently, my view of any situation or individual is influenced by – and my behaviors reflect – the coloring.

Minorities may refer to a numeric percentage as in the representation of People of Color in the executive ("C") suite. Minorities may also refer to people who, although they represent a numeric majority, are the *minority* in terms of power and influence. In many organizations women represent more than fifty percent of the workforce but less than twenty percent of the power and influence brokers. In both instances the term *minority* is useful. It is never used to connote inferiority or "less than" in value or importance.

Privilege – I use Peggy McIntosh's definition of privilege: "… an invisible package of unearned assets which I can count on cashing in each day, but about which I was 'meant' to remain oblivious. [It] is like an invisible weightless knapsack of special provisions, maps, passports, codebooks, visas, clothes, tools and blank checks."[vii]

Culture is the values, beliefs, norms and practices of a particular group that are learned and shared and that guide thinking, decisions and actions in a patterned way.

Cultural competency is the capacity to function effectively with groups and individuals from similar and different cultural systems.

The Questions

Every day, good and virtuous individuals who have intentionally or blindly stumbled into managing and leading others are faced with questions that test their personal and professional metal. These questions come from every part of the organization - the administrative assistant, the executive, the assembler, the engineer, the marketing manager and the salesperson. Individuals with titles of team leader, manager and supervisor are faced with challenges that weren't addressed in their university classes in the '80s, the management seminars they attended in the '90s or the in-house training provided last month.

How do you help the executive who comes to you and says, "I've done everything I can to motivate my managers to meet their diversity goals. Some of them seem to get it, but most of them don't. I really don't think it's because they don't want to; I just think they have a lot to do and it's hard to focus on this."

Or the senior manager who wonders, "Where do you learn how to pay attention to diversity without stereotyping? I'd like to find out what the issues in my group are, but I don't want the liability attached to it. I'm at a loss and have no idea where to go or even what I need."

What quick and pithy answers do you provide to the manager who asks, "Who do I go to with a diversity problem? HR doesn't have the answers, and legal says there's nothing they can do to help since it's not a policy issue. My senior manager doesn't know any more than I do."

How does the executive help her sales manager who slumps down in his chair, rubs his eyes and forehead and with quiet desperation says, "I'm at the end of my rope over performance issues with three of my five minority employees? I think the reason they are failing faster than others (non-minorities) is we've lowered our interview standards, but the customer still expects the highest level of service. I think we have to go back to hiring people based on talent and skill and not diversity."

If I hit F1 or F7 or F11 on my keyboard, will I have an answer for the angry and anxious manager who states, "We've been working on diversity for two years and instead of having more satisfied employees, we've got more complaints. No one's happy with what we're doing. What I really need is some help so I can do what I'm paid to do. I don't need more training."

Managing diversity and creating inclusion are new disciplines for many of us. With this new and evolving work come quandaries and pitfalls, solutions and debates that can be enlightening and frightening, not only for the leaders and managers, but for everyone involved. There's the concern voiced by the twenty-year employee who asks, "What kind of place is this becoming? No more jokes, no 'offensive' posters, which means anything fun or funny, our e-mail is being looked at and you have to watch every word you say or you'll offend someone and end up getting fired. We had a four-hour training session about a year and a half ago, and it didn't do any good. People left there feeling like they were better off never saying anything to anyone."

How do we deal with the worker who complains, "People bring a lot of differences to the workplace that belong outside. I don't talk about who I sleep with and don't want to know what anyone else is doing. Religion has no place in the workplace either. I don't understand why we have to let people leave early so they can practice their religion. I do mine on my day off."

Or the new employee who has been told by several of his colleagues, "Everyone knows why you were hired." He asks for answers. "I don't want anyone to think that the reason I got this job is because I'm Cuban. I'm not a person of color or whatever is politically correct. I'm just a damned good engineer."

Can we ignore the articulated or worse the unspoken, "I think this diversity stuff is a bunch of b-s. Everybody has the same chance to be successful here. If you fail it's because you're just not able to cut it. What should we do? Give someone extra credit because he's diverse? Well, when is it going to be my turn? Everybody has a day and a celebration but White men. All the time we're spending on these programs is costing us time and money."

What do we say to the single-no-children employee who feels like he is strapped with an increasing and never-ending workload because, as he tells us, "Three of my colleagues have taken maternity leave in the past year, and two others are pregnant? Women who leave to have a baby never come back the same. Their commitment, work ethic, everything is different and I have to pick up the extra work. Just because I don't have children they think I don't deserve any time off. Last week I told my boss I had to leave early to take care of my imaginary baby. He laughed, but I said, 'Hey it's the only way I get a break.' "

What book or quote do we offer the person who tells us, "My manager doesn't have a clue about managing diversity? She says she supports it, and in the same breath she tells a joke making fun of one of the gay men in our group. Her boss thinks she's on board, so what can I do?"

For many, it seemed like being successful was easier in the early '90s, before all of this talk about diversity. How do we help those who say, "I think the most difficult issue we face is style differences? Race, gender and those things don't matter here, but if you're not an analytic you'll never be successful."

For those who are duty-bound to get everyone to work together, how do they re-energize the employee who states, "The leadership says it cares about diversity, and yet there aren't any Blacks or Hispanics in senior management? It's all lip service. We just came back from a great training session on Asian culture. Too bad none of the managers showed up. They are the ones who really need this training. Why don't they ever show up at any of these events? I've been here for fifteen years, and nothing has changed. I'm not investing any time in this 'new' effort."

Or those who say, "We're all really just human beings. Why can't we all be treated the same, live by the same rules and forget about all these differences?"

A wonderful publisher who was reading my early draft asked, "Wouldn't you agree, the Fortune 100 have diversity and inclusion pretty much under control? They have highly paid diversity executives managing some pretty hefty budgets and staffs working on major corporate integration initiatives."

Well, yes, I'd agree they have some pretty hefty budgets and highly paid executives, but diversity and inclusion under control? No! Not even close.

Have you ever said (aloud or to yourself), "With all the money we've spent and all the time we've invested, why aren't we seeing the returns *they* (whoever they are) promised?"

This book is for all of you who have programs but don't have inclusive environments and are having difficulty figuring out why. It's for those of you who sit in the "C Suite" – at the highest levels of the company – and wonder how this many years on the diversity journey could end up here – at least two hundred kilometers from the land of milk and honey, fearing another dead-end road with lawsuits, infighting and dysfunctional teams.

How did we get here? Three roads converge. First, management does not feel prepared – trained, educated or fully supported. Second, employees are not confident that what the organization says it values and what it actually cares about are the same or congruent. Third, the value of diversity (differences and similarities) is not evident or understood by the organization or the individuals.

There's no magic potion or genie in a bottle. It's just you and I trying to address the myriad of questions, frustrations and concerns and at the same time energize and motivate those around us. The keys to getting everyone rowing in the same direction with determination, enthusiasm and passion are next.

The Combination

I ask that you think of the $^7K^2S$ as a combination to a safe rather than a set of door keys. The piece of paper with the combination written on it says you must go right to 44, left to 16, right to 18 (past 16) left to 3, right to 6 (past 3) and then left to 28. If you do only the first three numbers, you'll make progress, but it will not be very satisfying. To open it, to get to the treasure, you have to follow all of the instructions and use all of the keys.

Using the Keys

Millions of dollars, thousands of employee hours, significant and scarce resources have been dedicated to figuring out how to develop, maintain and address the challenges and opportunities of the diverse workplace. For years I have helped leaders in large and small organizations identify the "keys" to unlock the power and passion for diversity and inclusion in their organizations.

The keys are in a precise and deliberate order. It is similar to building a house – the plans specify the order and sequence. Finishing the roof before completing the foundation is not a disaster, but it not the most efficient process. The keys overlap – the first is connected to the second and so on.

There are seven of them, and completing the four you feel most comfortable tackling amounts to offering a customer a shiny new car that has no tires or steering wheel. It may look great, but it's worthless to the person wanting to take a road trip. In this book we will examine the **seven** ideas that can take **any** organization from confusion to success; guaranteed.

The Seven Keys To Success (^{7}K^{2}S) are simple. They are:

Key #1

There are clearly articulated links between the organization's success and the diversity and inclusion initiative or journey.

This is often called the business case for diversity. The essential words are *clearly articulated links*. People must see a connection between what we're asking them to do – learn, teach, lead, follow, change or behave differently – and a goal **they** see as beneficial, whether it's personal, financial, political or organizational.

Key #2

Leaders exhibit behavior that reflects a visible commitment to long-term systemic organizational change.

People don't do what we tell them to do. They do what we do. It takes seven to ten years to achieve a diverse and inclusive environment, so leaders' dedication has to be enduring. It's not about quick fixes; it requires diligence and a commitment to looking at everything in the organization, especially those things we value. Leaders' actions – the walk and the talk – must demonstrate their commitment to the journey, not the destination.

Key #3

There are individuals who provide strategic guidance and operational support to the leadership and the organization.

No matter how committed the leadership is they will need help. Diversity councils, employee networks, human resources and training and development are a few of these helping groups. The help can range from developing and monitoring goals and measurements to soliciting new marketing ideas from underserved consumer bases.

Key #4

There are clear success measurements and performance deliverables.

Organizations are intimately familiar with metrics. Regardless of the size of the organization, the work they do or the population they serve, all of our organizations measure things. Those things we measure are the things we value. As with any important endeavor, there must be plans, goals and measurements of progress and success.

Key #5

There are multiple learning and educational opportunities.

When it comes to diversity and inclusion, it is safe to assume that most people in our organizations need and want to be better educated and informed. It is also true that individuals learn differently. We must provide multiple opportunities for employees to develop their understanding and expertise in working in the cultural mosaic of today's workplace. Classroom, Internet, audio and video resources, speaker series, brown bag lunches, book clubs, networking events and external conferences are just a few of the ways we can learn and educate ourselves and colleagues.

Education has to address cultural competency and privilege. It has to provide skills for your hands and open your heart.

Key #6

Everyone participates.

The diversity and inclusion initiative will in some fashion touch every employee in every section – from the shop floor to the boardroom. This journey is not limited to the executives. Everyone has to have some "skin in the game," some investment in the success of the adventure and some active involvement along the way.

Key #7

The organization makes a leap of faith.

People often ask for *proof* that diverse and inclusive organizations are better. They want to see *concrete* and irrefutable evidence that their efforts will result in better numbers and statistics. In my early days at DEC, Barbara Walker said to me, "At some point, leaders have to make a quantum leap of faith, 'a belief in or trust in somebody or something, especially without logical proof.'"[viii]

No matter how much proof I offer you (and I will offer plenty throughout the book) at some point you have to take that leap and just believe that treating people well will lead to them staying longer and contributing more. You also must have faith that a wider bandwidth of solutions will come from a more diverse population and lead to better and more innovative ideas. If I'm wrong, don't hire me to help you. If I'm right (and I have thirty years of *proof* that I am), let me help.

Chapter two

vii

The Beginning

The first time I witnessed how these keys could help an organization create a diverse and inclusive culture was in 1980 – back in "the good old days" of Digital Equipment Corporation. Bill Hanson, vice president of manufacturing, embraced the notion that people work best when they feel valued. Maybe the fact that he was a Californian in an organization dominated at the top by men from New England heightened his sense that changes were imminent. (As early as the late '70s and early '80s the changes in the workforce were evident in California.) Perhaps the experience of the shifting demographic trends made it easier for him to see that the talent base was evolving from homogeneity to heterogeneity. Whatever it was, he brought a new approach to managing and leadership.

Although he and his executive team were extremely skilled in manufacturing technology, they were ill-equipped to tap into the diverse talent pool. To prepare his rapidly growing manufacturing organization for the future, he hired some of the best and most knowledgeable managing diversity and inclusion consultants in the U.S., including Dr. Price Cobb and Barbara Walker. I was lucky enough to join that group in January 1980, and for the next ten years I witnessed firsthand the struggles and victories of managers and leaders as they moved their organizations from groups of employees who appreciated their sameness to diverse and complex teams with language, style and visible heterogeneity.

In 1979 Ms. Walker instituted the process of "Core Groups" – multiethnic, multicultural gatherings of twelve to eighteen senior leaders and managers who agreed to spend one full workday a month for one year developing what Dr. R. Roosevelt Thomas terms *diversity matur-*

ity. Bill Hanson and his executive team led the way in this process. He was a working participant in the first DEC Core Group, and his leadership behaviors established the culture of learning that let the organization capitalize on the diversity in its ranks. It was Mr. Hanson's behavior that solidified my belief in the power of visible leadership.

Under his and others' leadership, DEC became truly a great place to work, with potential employees waiting for two to three years to join the company. In a time when technical talent was paid at the top of the scale, DEC employees stayed for midrange salaries. Ethnic minorities came from around the U.S. to live in areas with few minorities like Acton, Massachusetts (my daughter was one of three non-White children in the elementary school), and Burlington, Vermont. Did it's inclusive culture help the company to remain in business – for many very profitable years, yes, but ultimately business decisions related to products and architecture ended its reign, and the doors were closed. Even now, twenty years later, wherever I meet another ex-DEC employee the topic of conversation revolves around the beauty and power of that culture. Under the leadership of Hanson and many others there was a vision, leaders, support, education, metrics, participation and as Ms. Walker described it, "A quantum leap of faith."

Today, in order to achieve inclusion and diversity three conditions must accompany the seven keys. The journey or idea must be Visible, Inclusive, and Integrated (VII). The organization, from the C Suite to the mailroom, must be aware that the journey has begun, that we are all expected to join the parade, not just as spectators but participants, and that everything that touches our life will have a component of the journey.

The three conditions, Visible, Inclusive, and Integrated, are not optional if you want to reach your goal of a diverse and inclusive environment.

> Look for these three conditions in all of your work.
> Ask, ask and ask again:
> Is the work we're doing Visible (can be seen from every angle and view)?
> Is it Inclusive (welcoming to everyone)?
> Is it Integrated into everything we do and all that we are?
> **V**isible
> **I**nclusive
> **I**ntegrated

VII – Everything adds up to seven.

VII – Visibility

In a recent workshop someone asked, "How will we know if our diversity program is on the right track?" My answer was, "When every badge holder and every person on the payroll can comfortably and confidently answer this question: 'Why are we (at ABC Company) spending 10 cents or ten minutes on this journey?' "

The *right track* begins and ends with everyone in the organization understanding what we're doing, why we're doing it and how they and the company benefit from the success of the effort. The effort is immediately visible to employees, customers, clients, vendors and anyone who comes in contact with any part of the organization.

Why so much emphasis on visible? Because people do what they believe is important, and visibility is a tangible measure of importance. If you want to understand what an organization values, look at what it talks about both publicly and privately. I have always maintained that if managers paid attention to budget numbers only once or twice a year (the number of times diversity and inclusion is discussed in many companies) few if any organizations would successfully achieve their budget goals. Balance sheet numbers populate PowerPoint presentations, e-mails, memos, meetings and hallway conversations. It is visible because it's important and it is important because it is visible. No matter where an employee fits in the hierarchy, she will be aware of the importance of achieving the budget goals.

We are what we repeatedly do. Excellence, then, is not an act, but a habit. (Aristotle)

A Case Study – The Niontek[ix] Safety Initiative

In the mid-'90s I was working for Niontek. About six years before I arrived the leadership identified *Safety* as a major initiative. The information from the managers tracked safety issues and concerns and created a clear picture of the impact on employees. The company leadership defined the initiative as urgent because of its impact on profit, people and products. The more unsafe the environment, the more likely the company would experience quality issues with the product, medical and health liabilities, lawsuits from employees and loss of revenue in both measurable and assumed ways. The leaders assigned several of their most senior staff to develop what would become known as the Safety First Initiative (SFI). The name indicated the level of attention they were willing to devote; it was *safety first*. They allocated the resources of time, energy, dollars and focus.

One of the fundamental principles was that the importance of and the expected outcomes of the SFI would have to be visible to every employee. On every floor, in every building, in every state and every country there were safety prompts or reminders. The in-house publication ran reports and updates. At the public phone booth in the lobby of one of the thirty-plus buildings was a poster describing the importance of safe behaviors (a message for visitors, since most employees had access to company equipment). At each exit from the cafeteria was a large cardboard clown with a sign, "We're not clowning around; lids are required on all cups that leave here." In every training classroom were at least five signs that identified things you could do that would help you stay safe and keep others safe.

In the course of conducting one of my first diversity training sessions, I was leaning on the back of a chair while I spoke. During a break, an employee approached me and asked, "Would you please not lean on the chair back? It's really not safe." I was struck by her frankness and lack of concern about my reaction. She didn't hesitate or stumble, and she was not self-conscious asking a stranger to help with their safety initiative. This is important because often employees say they are not comfortable addressing others' behaviors – they don't want to seem like the diversity police.

I asked if she was on the safety committee or if ensuring that people were safe was a part of her prescribed job responsibilities. What she said surprised me: "No. I just know it's important for everyone to pay attention to safety." It was simple, straightforward and without apology or blame. As I began to ask questions of others in the organization, I discovered that the SFI was talked about in every morning meeting, the numbers of safety incidents were posted throughout the buildings, and employees were given rewards and recognition for pro-safety behaviors and practices. The SFI was an important element of the Niontek culture and was visible in everything they did.

How do you make the ^{7}K^{2}S journey visible? Do the obvious.

- Provide obvious symbols; posters, badges, signs, committees and more subtle messages that weave the theme into the fabric of every town hall, management meeting and employee gathering.

- Talk about it, write about it, make videos and show them in the cafeteria. Showcase it, point it out, acknowledge behaviors and practices that reinforce the journey and make it as common as money. If you want the ^{7}K^{2}S to be visible, every meeting has to have time devoted to discussing some aspect of the journey. It can be as specific as questions involving one of the Keys or a general conversation about a diversity-related opportunity.

- Provide rewards. They reinforce the behaviors that have been identified as supporting the journey. The rewards can be simple. Niontek gave coupons for free food and drinks in the cafeteria for behaviors like moving electrical cords when there was the possibility that someone could trip over them. Teams had free pizza Friday to celebrate achieving their weekly SFI goals. They can also be systemic – every Niontek manager had SFI goals in his/her performance evaluation. They can be financial – a lump sum amount of money or added to the bonus system.

Leaders ensure visibility!

Every week ask yourself and others:

- When is the last time *I/we* talked about the journey?

- Do my/our direct reports know which way we are headed and what needs to happen next?

- Is this journey a part of every message I/we deliver?

- If I am a new employee, how long will it take before I am aware of this initiative and its importance to our organization?

- Do our clients, customers, vendors and suppliers know how important this is to us, and are they clear about their responsibilities to help us achieve it?

- When I/we visit any of our buildings, is there a clear indication of the importance of this journey?

What impedes making the [7]K^{2}S journey visible?

At one end is apathy or "who cares" and at the other end is the fear that people will "tire" of hearing the same thing over and over – too little or too much.

Apathy – too little.

The lack of a will to do anything happens in companies that do not appreciate the value of the journey. Sometimes this is because nothing that seriously disrupts their life has happened (yet). In this case it's likely that you will hear, "If it ain't broke, don't screw it up." Or, "We have so much going on that this is just going to distract us from our *real* work." And the always popular, "Why start something that's just going to cause problems?"

At Niontek, there were people who initially (and some throughout the life of the journey) thought the SFI was a lot of effort dedicated to something that really was not a problem. After all, no one had been killed because of a safety incident, and initially there was little hard data to show how it would improve corporate profits. Additionally, it would be more work for people who were already stretched to the limit. The "no problem" notion can keep the initiative, whether it is safety or diversity, off the radar screen. This is the too-little scenario.

Fear – too much.

At the "too much" end is the concern that people will become immune to the message if they hear it at every gathering. People will get "sick of hearing about it all the time" and eventually will tune it out. They may even develop a negative response to the topic.

At StarrCom[x] I heard people talking about "diversity fatigue." When I asked what this meant, I was told that so many people were involved for so long, they were suffering from a new (and apparently serious) malady – diversity fatigue. One manager suggested we take a hiatus and give the people time to rest. "Then," he said, "we can start again."

Interestingly, the notion of "too much" never stops companies from talking about profits, time to market, market share, products and budgets. I've never heard a senior manager tell the CEO, "You know, my people are really tired of hearing about 'the customer this and the customer that.' " Or, "Let's take a break from all this focus on providing better service to our clients. We'll revisit it next year after people have had time to rest." Even if they think it, they don't say it. This is because the CEO and the executives have demonstrated that they have faith in the importance of these issues for the health and sustainability of the organization.

To keep the initiative visible and avoid the "too little or too much" concerns make sure each of the $^7K^2S$ are viewed as critical to the growth, development and continuance of the organization. Remember: People do what they believe is important, and visibility is a tangible measure of importance. *Visibility* is the first condition that must be present. The second condition is *Inclusivity*.

VII – Inclusivity

It is everyone's work.

The perfect train is one that can accommodate the diversity of its riders. This train will attract more regulars, bring in more revenue and be able to support upgrades, renovations, and immaculate and stylish cars. This train will be filled with cars that have seats for those who like to sit, areas that comfortably accommodate people in wheelchairs, handles for those who prefer or need to stand, poles for the kids who want to spin around and handrails within reach of the short rider.

If you are going to achieve the $^7K^2S$, the journey must be inclusive. Everyone must have a place on the train, a seat, a rail, a grip or a pole. This is important because for many U.S. organizations their introduction to diversity came from government interventions related to equal employment opportunity and affirmative action. These two important building blocks of diversity are in the minds of many people not inclusive, but rather exclusive, especially for middle-aged, able-bodied, White males, who make up the majority of the leadership in organizations.

If I can't dance it's not my revolution.

I have long maintained that any journey that leaves behind or does not tap into the majority of the leaders and financial backers is doomed to fail. Emma Goldman said, "If I can't dance it's not my revolution." I interpret that to mean, "If I'm not included I'm not going to put much energy into it." I tell my audiences that the framing by the affirmative action architects allowed 70% of the workforce to opt out of participating in the work of creating a level playing field for White women and racial minorities. The architects did not ensure that White men could dance in this revolution and see themselves as part of it, rather than apart from it. As a result, for many leaders and managers the diversity journey is mistakenly portrayed as another way of saying affirmative action; it is viewed as excluding the majority of the leadership. The diversity and inclusion journey is for everyone. The most effective way to move the needle is to have all employees participating fully in the struggle and the success.

Bring all voices into the room.

Inclusivity means all voices must be brought into the room. Today in many U.S. (and almost all international) organizations the practices and behaviors we historically labeled diversity have the added title of inclusivity – creating the opportunity for many (or all) voices and perspectives to be heard.

The advantage of inclusion.

A business environment that understands and appreciates diversity will be open to a man who earned his degree in "natural resource planning and interpretation," with an emphasis in marine resources and who has an idea for a cartoon character. That organization will listen as this strange person (he played the ukulele and sang a version of the theme song) talks about when he taught marine biology at the Orange County

Marine Institute in California, he noticed his young students' enthusiasm for the creatures that live in tide pools: sponges, starfish, octopi and crabs. Stephen Hillenburg is the man, and SpongeBob, a global icon and multimillion-dollar marketing project, was his idea. If Nickelodeon appreciated ideas in only the traditional form, from people in the traditional disciplines (he was not a cartoonist), it might have missed this million-dollar opportunity.

How do you make the ^{7}K^{2}S journey inclusive?

- **Base behaviors and practices on diversity and inclusivity in the broadest context**. The way you define "diversity" and how you design the initiative will determine whether it is inclusive or exclusive. That said, it is one of the most challenging aspects of the journey because it is difficult to reshape perceptions that have been influenced by thirty years of history. Remember, the definition of *diversity* is the characteristics we have in common (similarity) and those that are unlike others (differences) and *the impact* our difference and similarities have on our interactions. This definition lets everyone be included in the diversity and inclusivity discussion and journey. Because we are talking about how our differences and similarities influence and impact how I relate to you and how you relate to me, everyone can participate without guilt or shame.

- **Create an *inclusivity climate*.** Inclusivity climate refers to "an individual's perceptions of the organization's attention to diversity and inclusion issues, as reflected through human resource policies and procedures and [its] general attitude toward the value of a diverse workforce for organizational effectiveness" (Schnieder, Gunnarson & Miles-Jolly, 1994). Understand that the characteristics of race and gender are included in the journey, but ensure that they are neither the only ones measured nor the only ones viewed as important. When you talk about any of the seven keys, design the work in ways that let more employees lead, learn and drive toward success.

23

- **Seek participation from every segment of the population.** One of the most convincing examples of this came when I was working with a division of StarrCom that had a reputation for excluding ethnic minorities from leadership roles. The leaders were all White (a fact I pointed out, as no one seemed to want to see that as part of the challenge). We talked about ways they could change the perception of being a "Whites-only club." Change would let them get ideas and talent from a larger pool of candidates. They came up with several solutions, including developing relationships with organizations where the majority of the membership was multiethnic, conducting informational interviews with members from the targeted groups in the surrounding industries, mentoring ethnic minorities they identified as "high potential" and finally hosting a two hundred person networking event for eleven ethnic minority organizations. The division leaders listened to feedback and suggestions on ways to become more inclusive. They implemented cultural changes in their groups. The leaders created the inclusive climate – each of them became involved. The work included, but was not delegated to human resources and the employee networks. For many of these leaders it was the first time *they* had been asked to come up with a plan and actively participate in the implementation. They were able to change the culture, and it was *their* skills that were developed and valued.

What impedes making the $^7K^2S$ journey inclusive?

- **There's still unfinished business.** For some employees (primarily minorities) the broadening of the definition to include characteristics like leadership style, sexual orientation and religion may be seen as diluting the organization's efforts toward equity. They will often challenge inclusivity on the basis of "we're not finished with race and gender; how can we go on to add all of the other possible differences?" There is validity to this concern. Many organizations tire of the challenges of addressing biases and privilege related to race and gender, and embrace the broader definition as proof that they are "there." The leaders who may have felt excluded in the earlier phase of the journey quickly join the "it's much more than race and gender" parade without acknowledging the duality of the change process – it is about, but not exclusively about, race and gender. Leaders can respond by conceding that there is still work to be done to ensure that visibly diverse employees' concerns are addressed and keeping this on their radar.

- **Diversity is everything.** The other impediment is employees who will attempt to define inclusivity as code for *anything goes.* Here's how this behavior will appear. An employee is chronically late for work. The organization has written and communicated policies regarding work hours and consequences for tardiness. When confronted by the manager, the employee says, "Well, being late is just my diversity, and if the effort includes everyone else's diversity, why not mine?" It is imperative that management communicate that the policies and rules apply to all people without regard to their characteristics. Employees who are late regardless of their race, age or sexual orientation will face the same consequences. Another question you might hear is "If we value all diversity (which we have never said we do), does that mean we value thieves and murderers?" The answer is similar to the "tardiness" issue – No! Organizations have a set of fundamental human values like honesty (theft is cause for termination) and the valuing of human life. Labeling a behavior or a trait "diversity" does not make it part of every organization's values. Inclusivity is about inviting all employees to bring their talent, voice, knowledge and skills to the table to help the organization achieve its goals.

The third condition that must be present in all of the seven Keys is *Integration.*

VII – Integration

Years ago I attended an extraordinary exhibit of Chinese culture. Four floors of the museum were a treasure trove of sights and sounds from ancient and modern China. One of the most fascinating displays was an embroidery exhibit. Men and women stitched a design of an exquisite cat on one side, and when they turned it over, there was an equally beautiful design of a bird. Amazing! The embroiderers never turned the fabric over and looked at the back. I found out that this special process is called *double-side embroidery. The specific style of suzhou embroidery can be appreciated from both sides. Pictures look wonderful on both sides. The ends of silk threads are invisible. It is knitted in the right angle without piercing the other side. Both sides will present the same excellent effect.*[xi]

This is integration at its finest. The ends of the threads are invisible. When the goal for organizations is to have the diversity and inclusion work at its finest, it is impossible to tell where the initiative begins and ends. It's embedded in the fabric. What you see is an incredibly beautiful picture on both sides of the fabric.

All seven keys must be integrated into the fabric of the organization, woven through each aspect of the organization – vendor and suppliers, recruiting and retention, advertising and messaging, community and government relations, business practices, policies, procedures and culture.

Integration is central to a successful initiative. Historically, diversity and inclusion work is assigned to an adjunct department, e.g., HR, community relations or legal. The problem is people do not always bring their diversity - differences and similarities to the HR and legal functions. They bring all of themselves – their knowledge and skills, their culture, baggage, background and heritage – to every transaction. They bring them to the marketing meeting where those differences and similarities can contribute new ideas and a better understanding of the changing client or customer. They bring their diversity to the meeting between manufacturing and product safety and create better and safer products.

The threads of diversity and inclusion need to be evident in everything the organization does.

When we do not integrate diversity in the broadest context into our products, ideas and processes, we risk missed opportunities and mistakes.

- Buick named its new vehicle LaCrosse, which, in local Canadian slang, refers to masturbation. Even though they planned to sell the car in Canada, the Americans did not consult their Canadian counterparts. The Canadian division of GM announced it would choose another name for the vehicle when selling the car. "That was really a Canadian decision," said Pete Ternes, the director of public relations for GM's Buick Motor Division in Detroit. "We don't market [in Canada]. We focus on the U.S. market, and then the Canadian team will be responsible for how products are sold there." Nice answer, but unimpressive when you realize this snafu cost the company time, energy, focus and potential customers, and it could have been avoided.

- Abercrombie & Fitch made a costly mistake with T-shirts the company sent to and subsequently pulled from stores. The most offensive shirt featured "two smiling, slant-eyed gents with pointy bamboo rice-paddy hats, presumably the proprietors of the Wong Brothers Laundry Service. Their motto: 'Two Wongs Can Make It White.'"

- Pepsi used the tag line "Pepsi, the choice of a new generation" in its China market. In Chinese, this translated into "Pepsi, the drink that will awake your ancestors from the dead."

"We live in such a small world right now," said Andrew Erlich, the president of Erlich Transcultural Consultants. "When you get negative press, it's hard to make up for that."

These stories have occurred for centuries. Why are they more important to the business bottom line today? The world has shrunk. The time it takes for a message to go from the U.S. to China and back has decreased from days to seconds. A mistake or a mishap can have an immediate impact on the revenue and future of companies.

How do you integrate the $^7K^2S$ into the fabric of the organization?

Viewing all processes through the lens of diversity and inclusion.

- Recruiting – If a group or team is looking at increasing head count, it can look at *what's missing rather than who's at the table.* The team can ask how having someone with experience gained from working in another country would add important global focus. The group might discuss how having someone from outside the organization could prepare it better for future challenges or how having a woman on a predominately male team could be a benefit.

- Retention – Flexible policies and work-life balance initiatives allow more employees to participate. These initiatives should include single and childless employees, working parents and working caretakers, not just working mothers.

- Measurements – Tools must include the behaviors of managers, supervisors **and** individual contributors. The 7Keys Scorecard® (more in chapter seven) measures everyone in the organization. The Scorecard holds employees at all levels, in all departments, accountable for the success of the journey. Their contribution in helping the organization reach its recruiting and retention goals is as significant as their functional responsibilities. All employees should be expected to contribute their understanding of the emerging markets.

What can leaders do to improve integration of the $^7K^2S$?

- Look for opportunities to promote diversity and inclusion in "nontraditional" forums, e.g., discuss ways to incorporate diversity into the design of the cafeteria so that people are more likely to sit with others who are outside their usual circle.

- Imbed the diversity and inclusion message into employee and stakeholder meetings. (A quick check: Count the number of times diversity is mentioned in the last major communication.)

- Discuss ways for leaders to demonstrate their commitment to the journey in their daily work; they can put together teams with people from groups that don't typically work together on issues, e.g., a team with individuals from IT, finance and marketing to work on solving a quality control problem, or HR, sales and engineering to address the work space issue.

What impedes integration?

The definition of integrated is "bringing together processes or functions that are normally separate." This may be difficult for companies that are hierarchical, decentralized and those with extremely autonomous units. For example, it may be difficult to select leadership talent from parts of the corporation that are geographically or structurally remote. Extra effort will be needed to ensure that the leadership and measurement expectations reach all organizations and areas of the company.

Remember: Integrate all of the elements of the Seven Keys into marketing efforts, communications processes, community relations, services, recruiting and retention efforts, vendor and supplier relationships and the daily work life of employees.

As we examine the $^7K^2S$, keep the three conditions in mind (Visibility, Inclusivity, and Integration). The journey has to be visible to and inclusive of all employees, and integrated into every aspect of the organization.

Chapter three

key # 1 - the link

Business Case Motivation

The clearly articulated link between the journey and the achievement of business objectives (often referred to as the business case, although I believe it is much more than that) is the first key because:

A) If there is no connection between the organization's success and the journey, the trail will go cold when time and money become scarce. If we cannot answer the question, "What do we want to be great at and how can our initiative help us get there?" the initiative will fade and ultimately disappear.

B) The work of becoming familiar enough to clearly articulate the link between the life of the organization and the success of the work ensures that it is understood.

The link or connection is the nexus where a leader's unwavering belief in the significance of the diversity and inclusion journey meets the organizational realities of change. It is the intersection of the world, the workplace and the initiative. This link has to be real, tangible and visceral if the leader is going to be able to articulate how key diversity and inclusion are for the organization.

"In my mind, diversity is not a lofty ideal or philanthropic undertaking. It's about business results, economic investment, market outreach and corporate survival." Rick Priory, chairman and CEO, Duke Energy[xii]

Any journey that does not markedly help a company or group achieve important financial or program goals will be short-lived. Numerous costs are associated with the diversity and inclusion initiative and there have to be obvious gains to offset those costs. The benefits must be clear and compelling.

At the March 2003 Linkage Summit on Leading Diversity a survey revealed that 80% of Fortune 500 leaders see a strong correlation between their company's commitment to diversity and its long-term success.[xiii]

First Steps

Executives and senior leaders must:

- *Identify what they seek to achieve or avoid and how a diversity initiative can contribute.*
- *Be able to demonstrate to the organization how it will be better because it is engaged in the initiative.*
- *Develop clear success metrics that can be achieved through diversity and inclusion that might not have been achieved without it.*

Managers must:

- *Connect the diversity and inclusion journey to ways it will help them perform their jobs more effectively – to find, engage, lead, communicate with, develop and retain talent and create and maintain teams and groups.*
- *See how the journey helps them motivate their organization to accomplish their people, profit and/or service goals.*

Individual employees must see that the journey will help them:

- *Be more effective in their functional role.*
- *Feel more comfortable in the evolving workplace.*
- *Provide better service to the customer, and/or design a better product.*
- *Achieve their personal and professional goals.*

There are four major business case rationales that companies cite when talking about why they are spending money, time and resources on their diversity and inclusion journey.

They are:

> Fear and avoidance.
> Fairness and justice.
> Marketplace opportunities
> Workplace of choice.

We will explore each of these motivators and how they affect the business case. Because each one has a different fundamental underpinning, each will lead to different short and long-term outcomes and levels of success.

Fear and Avoidance

This business case is based on the assumption that a successful initiative will let us avoid costly lawsuits and the negative publicity that accompanies them. For many organizations, the diversity and inclusion journey develops from a strong desire to avoid negative events; harmful publicity caused by unhappy protected-class[xiv] individuals or groups that openly denounce the organization and/or sue the company and often receive large sums of money for past wrongs.

Few companies overtly embrace this as their motivation, but in workshops I've conducted when I ask the question, "Why is the organization doing this work?" the most consistent reason given by managers is "to avoid costly lawsuits and the negative publicity that goes with them." Even if the leadership does not openly state that this is the reason for the journey, it is communicated to the employees.

It often starts when an executive learns that an organization she identifies with by product or industry is or has been sued by an individual or group of employees. The employee groups publicly criticize the way they were treated and receive a large monetary award (i.e., U.S. Information Agency, $508 million; Milgard Manufacturing, $3.4 million; Ford Motor, $10.5 million; Texaco, $176 million; Coca-Cola, $192.5 million; American Seafoods, $1.25 million; Advantica (the parent company of Denny's), 54.6 million; R.R. Donnelley & Sons, $15 million).

The executive asks the HR manager, "Are we vulnerable to this kind of thing?" When she is told, "Yes," she immediately institutes a "diversity program."

Executives and leaders believe: The organization saves money if the initiative can help it avoid costly litigation.

Management believes: The diversity program (and that is what it is, a program) can help reduce an individual manager's liability.

Individuals believe: The program will lead to a less hostile environment with more sensitive management.

Pros

This motivation causes a significant amount of activity. It is a jolt. Fear is easily communicated. It's a recognizable emotion for most, if not all, employees. It's easy to stimulate activities and attention to the journey. Training is instituted. Money is available for activities. Employee networks flourish.

Talking about or describing what we don't want to happen takes less thought than deciding what we do want to see. For action-oriented, hierarchical and rules-oriented organizations, this business case motivation can be energizing. The senior leader says, "We will," and the rest of the organization lines up behind her. Everyone has clear marching orders: "Keep them happy."

Cons

Cautious, careful people, always casting about to preserve their reputations ... can never effect a reform. Susan B. Anthony

The avoidance motivation is the least effective business case rationale. It is a knee-jerk response to negative stimuli and doomed to fail to help the organization achieve any long-term sustainable business objectives. This is because fear is a short-term motivator, and it's difficult to develop work based on avoiding something that hasn't happened to us. After all, the other companies are not as smart as we are or they wouldn't make such stupid mistakes.

The types of activities you will see in the avoidance mode are: hiring and promotion targets (described in the organization as quotas and bounties). The new hires and other members of the "scary class" describe their experiences in these ways:

- *"My colleagues believe that the only reason I was hired is because I'm Black."*
- *"I was told by my manager that he had to hire a woman and I was the only one available."*

- *"When I was promoted, someone asked my manager why he chose me. He said (with me sitting in the room), 'I needed to hire a minority and Sheri fit the bill.' I was stunned and angry. He didn't mention my qualifications or the work I'd done for the company for the last seven years."*

- *"My assistant was told that she didn't have to worry because everyone knew I'd fail. After all, the only reason I was there was because the company was sued a few years ago and they had to hire women."*

Management is told that it cannot fire any of "them" without going through lengthy and complicated processes, which makes hiring "them" a frightening idea, but since the measurement and reward systems are based on doing just that, only the most powerful can refuse. The measurements and rewards involve how many of "them" you have and making sure none of "them" sue you. Without proper training, managers become resentful, fearful and reckless. They hire people who are likely to fail either on their own merit or because there's no support for them. These managers report:

- *"I was forced to bring in a minority with fewer skills, and when I tried to fire him because he wasn't able to do the job he sued us."*

- *"I'm being measured on promotions that just make my boss look good, but really don't help anyone. I've got angry White employees who feel cheated, and minorities who can't win."*

- *"It doesn't matter what you do. People will sue you because it's easier than working for money and we always pay them. It doesn't matter if we're right or wrong. HR and legal tell me it's cheaper to pay them than to fight it. Hell, I'm surprised more people don't sue us. I would."*

Under the fear and avoidance motivation, even managers who believe that it takes a jolt to get the organization to pay attention to diversity and inclusion find this rationale paralyzing. Instead of making their lives better by reducing their liabilities, it does the opposite – the initiative escalates their vulnerability. They see their colleagues making personnel decisions that are clearly doomed to fail. It's difficult to add reason to the mix when avoidance is the driver. Individuals on both sides of the "benefit" are unhappy with the initiative. The fear-and avoidance-driven initiative is difficult to advocate – it creates apprehension, anger and division.

Fairness and Justice

The fairness and justice business case is "characterized by a belief in a ... moral imperative to ensure justice and fair treatment of all members of society".[xv] (David Thomas)

Executives and leaders believe: It will create an inclusive environment by leveling the playing field.

Management believes: It will allow them to recruit and retain employees who are productive because they feel like they are (now) being treated fairly.

Individuals believe: It will ensure that everyone (especially those who have been historically excluded) will receive fair and equitable treatment.

As with the fear and avoidance business case, the fairness and justice approach is a bi-product of the legacy of affirmative action. In 1990, Dr. R. Roosevelt Thomas Jr. defined affirmative action (which looks very much like the fairness and justice business case) as "an artificial, transitional intervention intended to give managers a chance to correct an imbalance, an injustice, a mistake."[xvi]

This driver became "the right thing to do" diversity movement. Fifty-five-year-old White men were quoted in all of the important journals talking about why diversity was the right thing to do for their companies. "It's about time we gave everyone a chance." "We must level the playing field and make our company a true meritocracy." The emphasis was on the word "right," meaning just, fair-minded and equitable. The major focus was on recruiting and retention goals.

Pros

Who can argue with the fairness proposition? It's un-American to espouse a playing field that gives the home team a blatant advantage. If at the U.S. Open all of the U.S. tennis players were given an automatic one-set lead, the rest of the players would rebel. If at the Olympics the host country's soccer team started the game with a two-goal lead, the Olympic Village would riot. The "right thing to do" movement feels good. It is easy to rally people around acting in ways that are based on fairness and a level playing field. This business case invokes the words of Dr. Martin Luther King Jr.: "...that someday a person will be judged not by the color of his skin, but by the content of his character." The righteousness of the business case based on fairness and justice touches our hearts. We hear the sounds of choirs and see the faces of men and women we admire. The phrase I most often associate with DEC's founder, Ken Olsen is "Do the right thing." For DEC and many other organizations, diversity was and is the right thing to do.

Cons

There are two problems with the fairness motive: first, the definition; second, the timing.

The problem with using this as the foundation for the business case is that when resources become scarce and financial pressures increase, it's difficult to justify doing something today based on something you didn't do yesterday. Many people say they had no part in creating racial problems and perpetuating injustices. "I didn't discriminate against anyone, so I don't see why I should pay." Selling this to the larger organization is difficult. How do you effectively communicate the message that we're going to invest time, energy and money in a journey because our forefathers were prejudiced? It's the reason the discussion of reparations for slavery is so contentious.

Additionally, the organization continues with the initiative even when members of the organization feel like it is no longer needed – that the company is at last a meritocracy.

The additional burden placed on this business case strategy is that it doesn't demonstrate any future benefits. Being just and fair is beneficial in a religious or personal context, but it is much more difficult to quantify the benefits to an organization whose major challenge is beating its competition to the goal, whether that's charitable contributions for large nonprofits, patients for hospitals and medical centers, or consumers for automotive companies. As one executive said, "My shareholders don't give a damn if I'm fair; they want to see profit."

It is also difficult to sustain the "right thing" approach. There comes the day in every organization's life when some people believe that the playing field has been leveled, others are not sure and some are convinced that there are miles to go before the playing field is close to level.

"We don't see things as they are; we see things as we are."
Anais Nin

There are two additional frameworks to describe the business case for diversity and inclusion – marketplace opportunities and the workplace of choice. Both of these have a better chance of sustainability and long-term success than either the fear or fairness cases. I present them separately and then as connected. The most compelling business case argument will emphasize that the changes in the marketplace *combined* with highly satisfied employees will yield the highest returns on the resources dedicated to the diversity and inclusion journey. Their strength is in the combination.

Marketplace Opportunities

This is the easiest business case to sell: the link between an organization's success and its ability to capture new and expanding markets, clients and customers. The data is irrefutable.

- The combined buying power of African Americans, Asian Americans and Native Americans in 2007, according to the Selig Center's findings, should be more than triple its 1990 level of $453 billion, totaling almost $1.4 trillion.

- "The Gay & Lesbian Market: New Trends, New Opportunities" says buying power for the gay/lesbian/bisexual/transgender (GLBT) market in 2002 is estimated at $451 billion and projected to reach $608 billion by 2007, a cumulative increase of more than 34 percent from 2002 figures.

- German Chancellor Gerhard Schröder said he feels it will be possible to double the volume of German-Chinese trade to a level of $100 billion before 2010.

The marketplace opportunity motivation requires understanding the demographic changes that affect your products and services.

- The telecommunications industry realized that Latinos, the largest minority, were underserved. The industry dedicated millions of dollars to understanding that market using internal (employees and customers) and external (advertising and focus groups) channels.

- The banking industry changed hours of operations in different population areas as it became aware of the unique banking patterns of the 21st century consumer.

- Hospitals and medical facilities recognized medication reporting methods that were different based on cultural habits. The facilities realized that for some patients herbs might not be considered "medicine" when a physician asks if the patient has been taking any "medication," so the intake forms were modified.

Pros

The global marketplace lets companies capture broader market share and explore profits in areas that were previously invisible to them. This strategy is extremely valuable for companies with global connections and requirements. It is also an easy strategy to explain to the board of directors, shareholders and the financial community. Lastly, the workforce can easily recognize the importance of the changing marketplace. From hospitals to the automotive industry to MTV, from the streets of Beijing to the avenues in Buenos Aires, diversity is influencing corporate behaviors.

Cons

Alone (without the workplace of choice) this strategy can seem singularly focused on profit, with little respect for the people who do the work. For example, if the consumer giant LaMaxxe[xvii] Inc. focuses on attracting Hispanic dollars but does not have Hispanic and Latino employees or has a negative reputation with its Hispanic employees, the marketplace opportunity business case will seem hollow and hypocritical – focused on profit at any cost. This could lead to a backlash that could negatively impact the organization's revenue.

Workplace of Choice

The 1987 Hudson Institute Report for the U.S. Department of Labor, "Workforce 2000," showed that the demographic landscape of the U.S. is changing so dramatically that the average White male manager who thinks there will be plenty of White male clones to hire will be shocked to encounter a room full of [people of color] (Stewart, 1995).

Not only was the Institute report shocking, but it was followed by the challenge of retaining, engaging and fully utilizing this new workforce. The more companies employed the diverse workforce, the clearer it became that if an organization hoped to remain viable and vibrant, its culture would have to become friendly and welcoming to a wider variety of employees and customers. Companies also realized that retaining talent was necessary since turnover costs range from 150% to 300% of an exempt employee's annual salary.

You do the math. If your organization has 3,000 employees with an average salary of $18,000, (about $8.75 per hour) an annual turnover rate of two percent (60 employees) costs approximately $1.6 million per year, assuming that turnover is limited to non-management personnel. You say, "That's too high; turnover can't cost that much." Turnover is much more than replacement cost. It is:

> Recruiting +
> Training +
> Learning curve +
> Knowledge lost +
> HR/legal/accounting +
> Management time +
> Management focus +
> Lost influence and relationships +
> Decreased productivity of the group =

1.5 times the annual salary for staff and 2.0-3.0 for managers.

Today executives, leaders and managers realize that the employees who can help them achieve in the increasingly complex and competitive world no longer represent a single race, ethnicity or gender. It is clear that there are many uniquely positive outcomes from this new workforce – from diversity.

"The existence of a conflict of ideas has been shown to produce substantially higher quality solutions in diverse teams. A diverse team may have access to greater informational networks through their external communication channels" ("Managing Diverse Work Teams: A Business Model for Management," Sammartino, O'Flynn & Nicholas, 2002).

Pros

When organizations demonstrate that their business case for diversity and inclusion is their desire to be the workplace of choice and ensure that the changing workforce (women, different ethnicities and nationalities, people with physical disabilities, employees with different first languages and those with geographic diversity) has access and feels included, the results are an energized and productive employee base.

Satisfied employees deliver better customer service, are more engaged, provide more referrals and are less likely to choose voluntary termination leading to lower turnover cost and higher return on your people investment.

Want proof? Look in the mirror. Each of us remembers a job where we felt used and abused. For me it was a not-for-profit training program. I was by title the program director, but the executive director developed and owned the program. He was an abusive manager, who completely ignored my knowledge and my desire to contribute. The result - I found every excuse to avoid coming to work, leaving as early as possible and contributing the minimum required to keep my job. I thought it would get better, but it just got depressing. I physically left after two years. Emotionally I was out of there after six months.

On the other hand, when I worked at DEC I was blessed with three managers who treated me with dignity and respect. Not only was I physically there for a decade, but also I was emotionally and intellectually committed to the organization's success for the full ten years. The difference between my output, energy and focus at DEC and the program director position was the difference between working for a workplace of choice and being paid to show up at an intolerable job.

The Workplace of Choice delivers satisfied employees who are more engaged, provide more referrals and deliver a higher return on your people investment.

Cons

If the link is based solely on a workplace where everyone on the inside is happy, without a focus on the external – the customer, client, business and/or products – the company will end up with excited but unemployed people.

Marketplace/Workplace

It's no doubt in my mind that the broader the scope of perspectives, the broader the scope of success. Differing opinions give our products a broader appeal, attracting a larger customer base." Dieter Zetsche, *CEO, Chrysler Group, DaimierChrysler*

When leaders fully understand the marketplace and workplace business case motivations, it is easy to articulate the connection between the organization's diversity and inclusion journey and the ways an energized and satisfied workforce provides access to new markets.

How can your diversity and inclusion journey help you expand your market presence or help you attract and retain talent?
The LaMaxxe Example

In the early '90s the gay and lesbian network at LaMaxxe Inc. identified the GLBT consumer base as an underserved market that was a perfect fit for several of the company's major lines of business. As the senior managers in each line of business looked into this, they realized significant revenue and substantial positive reputation gains could come from understanding this emerging market segment. It was also clear that none of LaMaxxe's competitors were paying attention to this group, making entrance into the marketplace easy and inexpensive. LaMaxxe experienced considerable revenue growth with this new partnership and continues to use this example to show how the diversity and inclusion initiative can affect the company's ability to remain a winner in a very competitive environment.

The Airwelt[xviii] Example

Murali, an employee of Airwelt, a global manufacturing company, was visiting his parents in India. He and his wife had immigrated to the U.S. in the early '80s, and he made an annual trip home to visit family and, as he said, "to get some home-cooked meals." While he was there he noticed that his uncle was using a competitor's product in his factory. Murali was curious and asked why his uncle's firm was not using the product made by Airwelt. His uncle explained that when he was taking bids on the product, no one from Airwelt responded to his request for pricing and availability. "Furthermore," his uncle said, "The other company sent several salespeople to talk with me and other small businesses in the area." His uncle went on to explain that he called the Airwelt plant and told its officials that his nephew worked for the company, but the only thing he received from Airwelt was a brochure.

Murali contacted Jeff, his manager, in the U.S. and asked if he could extend his stay for one week to work with the local Airwelt offices and try to develop some business leads. His manager granted the time, contacted the India plant manager, made the introductions and offered to support the India office in any way he could.

The Airwelt India plant was able to write contracts with several midsize businesses (including Murali's uncle) and capture a share of the business (increasing profits) that it previously missed. An additional benefit was a change in Airwelt's reputation from an unresponsive organization to one that was receptive and easy to work with. Another bonus: Murali is a highly satisfied and motivated employee.

Jeff later told Murali that he knew that having employees with diverse cultural backgrounds would pay off, however he never dreamed it would be this way. "But," he said, "When you called me I knew your knowledge of the local area combined with your understanding of our products and services would lead to something good."

Jeff and Murali presented their learnings and ideas as a case study to the leadership team and recommended that Airwelt form an International employee group to discuss ways to increase business in their home countries. With the help of the Executive Diversity Council, they created a global/local panel that meets annually to explore ideas for sharing knowledge and best practices and improving business results.

Do you have untapped resources? There are an abundance of examples like these two. They illustrate the link between the Marketplace Opportunities and the Workplace of Choice. Employee networks and individuals like Murali can help your organization and individual business units overachieve on their financial and market goals, become the company of choice for consumers and provide excellent client and customer service.

Choosing The Business Case

Organizations and groups choose the business case that best suits their culture and stage of the journey. These four business case choices are not mutually exclusive and may be evolutionary or sequential – an organization may begin at the Fear and Avoidance and progress to viewing the business case as an expression of Fairness. This organization may subsequently see the benefit of capturing an expanding marketplace and/or being the workplace of choice. It is also true that there are organizations that begin and end their journey with a single business motivation.

Although I believe it is ideal to have an integrated workplace of choice/marketplace-based vision, this may not be best for your organization. Regardless of your choice – fear and avoidance, justice and fairness, marketplace or workplace of choice – remember that the initiative must be *Visible, Inclusive and Integrated.*

Keeping it visible.

Everyone should be able to answer the question, "Why are we spending one hundred euro or one hour working on this initiative?" The majority of organizations that "get in trouble" with their initiative have failed to build a solid business case and ensure that it is visible throughout the organization.

Remember:

People do what they believe is important, and visibility is a tangible measure of importance. If you want to understand what an organization values, look at what it talks about publicly and privately.

Make it visible:

- ✓ Talk about it at every opportunity – town halls, corporate meetings, executive retreats.
- ✓ Make it a part of the decision-making processes.
- ✓ Insure that at every level employees understand what the business case is and what the motivation for it is.
- ✓ Make its importance obvious – posters, rewards, discussions, and leaders' behaviors.

In your definitions and discussions ensure that your business case is inclusive. Inclusivity is more than talk; it's talk and walk. It will be evident in what you pay attention to, what gets measured and rewarded.

Integrate the reason for the initiative into all parts of the organization, including:

- ✓ Your staffing and retention policies and practices.
- ✓ Your products and product designs.
- ✓ The organization's marketing and sales initiatives.
- ✓ The service delivery systems.
- ✓ Company and group communications.
- ✓ Individual and team performance metrics.

Business Case Recipe

How do you get at the information you need to develop a cogent and powerful business case in order to clearly articulate how the initiative and the organization's success are linked? Ask your people!

Here's a recipe for a great business case.

The first part of the recipe will take four to six hours – enough time to think, but not so much that anyone is bored. Additionally, you will need one to two hours for the presentation and two to three hours for follow-up.

The ingredients:

Twenty-five to forty bright employees from the broadest possible cross-section of the organization.
One to two facilitators.
A large room with space for groups of eight to ten people.

The process:

- Bring all of the ingredients together.
- Gather ideas from the participants and place them into mixing bowls.
- Mix and blend the groups often so that people are continually being energized by new information from different people.
- Allow ideas to marinate while gathering new ones.
- Strain the answers to get to the meaty ideas.
- Have a few tasters test to make sure it's not too spicy, salty or sweet for the culture.
- While they're still warm, serve them with passion to the leadership.
- Thank the cooks!

One group followed this recipe and came up with a practical and effective tool to help division leaders develop their business case – to answer the question, "Why are we spending 10 cents or ten minutes on diversity and inclusion?"

The group asked leaders to think about everything through the filter of: What impacts our ability to achieve our people (recruiting, retention and motivation) and profit (return on investment, cost of doing business and customer retention) goals. Here is a sample of the questions the group posed.

Internal/People

- What do people value/care about and how could understanding this impact our business?

- What are employees' perceptions of our current environment and how do those perceptions affect achieving our goals?

- How would a safe environment for people to be "out" (e.g., GLBT, single parents, disabled, over 50) benefit our business?

- How does the communication stream between management and employees impact how people feel?

- How do our insider/outsider dynamics (such as people in different locations, e.g., U.S. and non-US, native and immigrant) impact productivity, people and profits?

- What will ensure that increased diversity (people with different work styles) will help people work together better?

- How does the ability to attract and retain talent impact business goals?

- What is the turnover rate? What contributes to it? What are the costs associated with it? How will diversity positively impact retention and ultimately decrease cost?

External/Profit

- How does the public view us and how does this impact our diversity and inclusion effort?

- Would a more diverse vendor/supplier pool impact our business and how?

- What business opportunities are we missing if we don't serve a diverse audience? Now and in the future?

- Which diversity business practices help attract opportunities (new products, marketing opportunities)?

- Are there options to grow our business by targeting diverse customers?

- Are our competitors missing a particular customer or market?

- How do we manage our diversity and inclusion efforts to create a positive external image?

- How can we leverage diversity and inclusion to create better/more profitable products?

- What has to be true if diversity and inclusion are to help us minimize our down risks (i.e., lawsuits, penalties/fines, advertising to combat bad imaging)?

- How can we use our diversity and inclusion initiative to gain a competitive advantage?

- How can diversity help us open up new markets?

- Will niche advertising increase profitability?

- What is the financial impact of diversity outreach?

Five most common planks of a business case:

1. Identifies future needs.
2. Is built around cultural ability/reality.
3. Is compelling.
4. Is a living document that evolves with the organization.
5. Drives all of the behaviors, programs and practices.

Tips for Connecting to the Business Case:

- *Provide ways for employees and groups to present information that can help the company or division achieve success.* At meetings and gatherings ask for ideas and experiences that can help the organization with challenges. You can solicit their ideas in open settings and in one-on-one meetings. Remember to give them feedback.

- *Train management personnel to solicit innovative ideas from "unlikely" places.* Encourage managers to role-play interactions. This is especially helpful when working with employees they do not usually associate with.

- *View groups and individuals as cultural business knowledge experts.* The more you know about cultural diversity, the more you will know what you do not know. Remember that people generally have more information about their own culture than others and are often willing and happy to share their knowledge.

- *Capture and publicize examples of how diversity and inclusion help your organization achieve hard and soft targets, people and profit goals.* Publicize achievements that illustrate the connection between the journey and business goals. Your internal online and hard copy newsletter is a good vehicle. It is important that employees see evidence that supports the organization's reasons for investing in the diversity and inclusion journey.

- *Celebrate wins that come as a result of your diversity and inclusion efforts.* Have "Achievement" parties when groups use their diversity to achieve business wins. At town halls, management meetings, conferences and staff gatherings acknowledge and reward the behaviors you want people to exhibit.

- *Recognize the limitations of your motivation choice.* Choosing the fear or justice rationale may be a valuable initial strategy. Both business cases can be energizing, but may not be the best long-term strategy. Be aware of the pros and cons for your choices.

OK, you've selected the business case model that works for your organization. What's next? It is imperative that the second turn you make, the second key you use – is leadership. The leadership's commitment to the journey is crucial to its success.

Leadership is not everything, but it is the second most important thing. *What is it* and *How do I get it* are next.

Chapter four

key #2 - leadership

Leadership is not so much about technique and methods as it is about opening the heart. Leadership is about inspiration – of oneself and of others. Great leadership is about human experiences, not processes. Leadership is not a formula or a program. It is a human activity that comes from the heart and considers the hearts of others. It is an attitude, not a routine.

Lance Secretan, Industry Week,
10/12/98

Spitting on the Floor

I was giving a talk to 250 senior managers for a major retailer at the invitation of the Human Resources manager and the company president (we'll call him Jim). Here's what I said: "I find it strange that people don't spit on the floors in your hallways. They don't while walking to the cafeteria turn their head to the side and spit into the potted plants or on the carpets. Now people do spit on the streets. I've seen them spit while walking in the parks, in the parking lots of malls, in the subways, on the streets, and on the mounds and in the dugouts at baseball parks. I'm a runner, and I've seen them spit on the streets while running a 10K, but never in my 27 years working with corporate America have I seen anyone spit on the floor during a staff meeting.

"I know that it's not because it's against policy. Without even looking I'm confident that spitting isn't mentioned in your Personnel Policy manual. So why don't people do it? I think it's because they've never seen any of you – the executives – do it. None of you have taken a pause during a budget presentation to spit on the floor (hopefully missing everyone's newly shined shoes) and then continued as if nothing happened. I believe that if one of you gathered a wad saliva and deliberately spit, that everyone in the room would give you immediate and negative feedback.

"I also firmly believe that if Jim, your president, did it at the beginning of every meeting and during the coffee breaks that within two years you would have a company where people routinely spit on the floors in meetings and in offices. This is because people do what their leaders do (or don't do). They do what the people with power do."

Leadership – The Importance of Footprints

People have asked me why certain leaders "get it." Why they never seem to waver in their commitment to creating a diverse and inclusive culture. The question has always fascinated me. In 27 years while working with executives and leaders in the financial, manufacturing, technology and entertainment industries I've come across five or six heterosexual, able-bodied, educated White men who "get it." I focus on White men for three reasons: 1) I know that when people ask the question, "why do some get it?" the image in their heads is White and male; 2) I believe that for people of color, White women, GLBT and disabled leaders, the challenge of identifying why they get it is colored and enhanced by their place in society; and 3) About sixty-five percent of managers and eighty-six percent of executives are White men.

The question of why some White men get it and the unasked question of why thousands of others don't is a mystery I will try to decipher or at least I'll provide some clues to help you solve it.

Here's what I know: The answer cannot be as simple as genetics. Many of the White, male, heterosexual and able-bodied leaders I've worked with have talked about their siblings and relatives who ridicule their diversity efforts. They express surprise that they grew up in the same environment with people who are determined to maintain the status quo – are comfortable with homogeneity and see no reason to change. Some grew up in homes with fathers or mothers who were social workers, others with parents or guardians who were mill workers or bankers. There is no pattern that helps answer the question "why?"

If genetics do not answer the question, is it possible that having power is what leads an executive to commit to the journey? No. There are numerous examples of executives who find the topic of diversity and inclusion frightening, and although they may say the right words, their behaviors indicate a reluctance to explore the intersection of power, privilege and equity.

Ask Chief Diversity Officers to give you examples of when and how their CEO or senior executives demonstrate their commitment to diversity and inclusion and you'll likely hear many more examples of when they did not. Power is not the determinant. If you don't believe me, read this.

Power Corrupts

I was asked to conduct a cultural audit for a large Mid-western manufacturing company. The company prided itself on having one of the more impressive diversity initiatives. There were networks, their business model was global and their re-cruiting strategy included historically Black colleges and universities (HBCUs). They had employees in the Midwest, on the West Coast as well as in several countries in Asia and Europe. The HR manager said the CEO and his team were committed to creating the most inclusive culture possible and needed help developing their training and education program.

I began by conducting an audit to help me understand the culture and identify what type of educational intervention might work best. The audit design was extensive – including paper surveys and questionnaires, focus groups and individual interviews with a cross-section of employees. The deeper I got into the audit the more concerned I became. One issue that sur-faced in every instrument and interview was the issue of trust. People did not trust the leadership; the managers and supervi-sors did not trust each other, the employees or the executive team; and the executive team did not trust one another. The company had several employee networks, including an African American and a gay and lesbian employee network. My inter-views with members of these two networks heightened my concern. I heard over and over "You can't trust HR and you can't trust management." The issue of trust felt like a mist that kept everything in the organization damp and slippery.

I took my findings first to the CEO and then to his executive team. In my one-on-one the CEO told me that trust was not an issue in his company and that my findings were incorrect. In the larger group when I shared the data and specifically mentioned the gay and lesbian network the CEO said, "I didn't know we had a gay group (although I mentioned it in my one-on-one). I want to know who they are and where they work." He chuckled, "They won't be working here any longer." None of his senior managers, including the head of human resources, said a word. As I looked around the room, I noticed that the executives were either smiling and looking at the chairman or staring at the floor. I said to him, "You have the power to create an incredibly diverse and rich culture here. You've got wonderful people who want to contribute, but they're afraid, not just hesitant, but seriously afraid to be openly who they are." "Well," he said, "If they're gay, they should be afraid." It never dawned on the CEO that I might be a lesbian – he offered me a very lucrative contract to come in and "get everyone trained.".

I refused to take the contract because a) I believe that even if you do not have the CEO's blessings you can't be successful if you've got the CEO's curse. During the final meeting I had with the HR manager he told me that his CEO "really did believe in diversity, he's just not good at showing it." And b) the road to hell is paved with good intentions and lucrative contracts.

In the end, the company lost talented, irreplaceable human resources, market share (it was unable to solve a product problem in Europe, perhaps because people did not share their solutions with others or seek the input from diverse perspectives), developed a negative reputation in several communities, which hurt their college recruiting effort, and is limping along.

It is not genetics – too many of you have brothers and sisters who don't get it and don't understand why you do. It is not simply having power – some who have it use it wisely and others do not. If it is not genetics or power that makes some executives better able to create an inclusive environment, what is it?

"I've done everything I can to motivate my managers to meet their diversity goals. Some of them seem to get it, but most of them don't. I really don't think it's because they don't want to; I just think they have a lot to do and it's hard to focus on this."

This is a frequent question from CEOs and executives. They genuinely believe they've done everything possible. I will frame the answer to focus on how their behaviors do or do not leave footprints for others to follow.

I will focus on two archetypal leaders, "Phillip" and "Victor." Phillip and Victor are not individuals, although I will refer to them as if they are. They are a type of leader, someone with power, influence and the ability to reward and punish the people who work for them. They also have the ability to significantly impact the culture and the workplace. They may be heads of departments, executive vice presidents, CEOs, functional directors or plant managers. They may work in technology, consumer products, medicine, manufacturing or finance. What they have in common is their ability to demonstrate their commitment to long-term system change, thereby helping achieve a visibly diverse and inclusive environment.

Phillip is the leader who provides the energy and passion for the journey. His footsteps are deep and large – making it easy for others to see and follow.

Victor is on the journey because he does not want to be seen as against it. Victor has what Steven Covey calls "secondary greatness – that is, social recognition for [his] talents, but [he] lacks primary greatness or goodness in [his] character."

What Drives Phillip & Victor?

Phillip is driven by the desire to be the best – at leading, following, learning and communicating. For him, the parts of the organization and the whole of the organization are one and the same. If one part fails the other parts cannot succeed. It's the "all for one and one for all" view. He wants people to describe the organization as a *great* (not just good) place to work, and he wants that to have meaning to people, to be much more than a cliché. He is driven by how people feel about and talk about the company.

In his personal life he embraces diversity. He has traveled extensively and lived outside his home geography. He gets fulfillment from being around people who are different from his "usual" world. Bill Hanson says one reason he left California and moved across the U.S. to Massachusetts was "As a family, we wanted to expand our knowledge of the U.S. and to better appreciate the values and history of New England [and] we wanted to know why Easterners talked funny."

One of the most phenomenal leaders I've ever worked for is Tom Freston, co-president of Viacom. Tom has lived and worked for extended periods of time in places where he was a minority and often talks about how that shapes his dedication to an inclusive culture. He has consciously lived through the difficulties and the advantages of being different. He says, "As a young adult, I was driven – consciously and subconsciously – to spend time living and working in several far-flung places around the world, including India and Afghanistan, because I longed to experience other cultures and ways of thinking. I got a feel for the excitement and rush associated with being around people who are very different from my own background and experiences, and I think I still carry with me that appreciation for otherness and multiculturalism."

Like Phillip, Tom Freston believes that what he does inside the organization will impact the world outside and what he learns from the world outside can help him effectively manage and lead inside. He is convinced that fairness and justice are the dominion of business. He is aware that his actions can in fact change the course of history.

Victor wants to be viewed as a powerful, connected and important executive with a supremely successful organization. He is driven to excellence by his ego and position. Being seen as a winner is his motivation, and he works tirelessly to achieve this. For Victor the workplace is his playing field. He surrounds himself with a homogenous group of people whom he trusts – those with a long history with him and subordinates who will do whatever it takes to make his organization successful. The reason he surrounds himself with homogeneity is not entirely race or gender based (although it contains elements of bias and prejudice); it is as much about his fear of failure and his risk aversion. He is risk averse where diversity and differences are concerned. For Victor I define risk as the distance between perceived differences. The more similarities (class, background, gender, race, education, etc) the lower the perceived risks; the fewer the similarities the greater the perceived risks.

He is a superb chess player, always looking for opportunities to increase the size and scope of his sphere of power and continually on the lookout for ways to bolster his reputation. Because diversity and inclusion bring complexities, interactions and interpersonal conflicts that do not necessarily respond to intellectual explanation and may require emotional investments, he is reticent to have more than a few uninitiated people in his top tier.

He is an "organization man" who will take on large, difficult and arduous work loads and expects his staff to do the same. This selflessness makes him a valuable asset to the organization; for he can always be counted on to do whatever it takes to live up to his commitments.

These are the characteristics I believe contribute to a leader's ability to "get it":

> Leaders are role models.
> Leaders acknowledge privilege.
> Leaders exhibit courage.

Leaders Are Role Models

"Example is not the main thing in influencing others. It is the only thing."

(Albert Schweitzer)

Leaders must demonstrate a passionate belief in inclusivity. They are seen as the example for appropriate actions. Employees seldom do what they are told to do; they do what the person they want to impress or emulate does.

This is why the second of the Seven Keys To Success – Leaders Demonstrate Their Commitment to Long-term Systemic Change – is vital.

What you do, how you behave, means much more than what you say. The demonstrated commitment to change is evident in the routine and daily behaviors of leaders and managers.

I use the term "leader" to refer to a combination of power, the ability to influence the behavior of others and status or hierarchy in the organization – those with the authority to "direct others by showing them the way or telling them how to behave" (Webster's).

The term "leader" can represent titles – vice president, director or plant manager. Or it can reflect responsibilities – diversity council leader or HR - people generally acknowledged to have power and status in the organization. Many leaders are managers. Some leaders are individual contributors and consultants.

All managers are leaders – not necessarily good leaders or conscious leaders or even willing leaders, but they are leaders – people who have the power and status to influence the behaviors of others.

57

Like raising a child, it takes a village to develop, nurture, support and build the leaders who can make long-term significant change. The leader doesn't move mountains by his muscle or vision and insight, but I believe he must make visible footprints on the journey – in the sand, the tar or the cement.

"Consider how hard it is to change yourself, and you'll understand what little chance you have in trying to change others."

(Jacob M. Braude)

Phillip starts with himself and works outward. He spends time listening and talking to an ever widening group of people. He has a reputation for being easy to talk with. He works to develop his "flat sides" (weaknesses) and is open to learning new and sometimes uncomfortable things. He puts himself in difficult situations in order to facilitate his growth.

Victor is not comfortable being asked to look inward or in the mirror. It sometimes seems that he views introspection as a waste of time, a touchy-feely activity that does not pay any business dividends. This may be due to his belief that there is a solid line separating business and personal, that the decisions he makes **inside** the workplace are not influenced by his life **outside**. He may give money to charities, but it is part of his corporate image – the result of his position. If he joins an organization, it will be one that mirrors his view of the world, seldom one that makes him uncomfortable.

The difference between Victor and Phillip is the willingness to accept responsibility for his impact on the environment.

"Expertise, for all its strengths, can make it more difficult to break out of established patterns of thought."

(Frans Johannson)

Victor listens to people of color leaders explain how they are excluded from many of the processes that lead to senior positions. With graphics, antidotes and direct experiences, they explain how they often feel excluded, the lone voice at the table, and spotlighted again and again. Victor says quietly to his managers, "I think they're exaggerating. It can't be that bad. I've never seen that happen, and I've been here fourteen years."

He responds to the group with dismissive body language and silence. He suggest to the other managers after the group leaves that "they probably have a point, but it's a few isolated incidents." That translates to "it is a tale told by an idiot, full of sound and fury, signifying nothing" (Shakespeare's Macbeth).

Victor is comfortable with the belief that the lack of diversity (gender, age, disability, style, pick one or two or more) is easily and honestly explained by the phrase "there just aren't any – and if there are two or three they're already working somewhere else."

When employees who can prove beyond any doubt that the organization mistreats them because of their age, race or gender sue the company, Victor never, regardless of the evidence, concedes that his behaviors have any influence on the environment. "Hey, I can't be responsible for the way my managers behave; one bad apple rots the barrel," he says dismissively. This is the act of digging a riverbed for denial.

Phillip, on hearing the tales from the people of color leadership group, immediately investigates the allegations. He starts from the perspective that talented, loyal employees seldom exaggerate, and generally minimize the negative. He calls on all of his leaders to take a critical look into their practices and procedures, to uncover potential and actual exclusionary treatment. He is committed to examining and, where needed, to changing "the way we've always done it."

Leaders must demonstrate a commitment to long-term systemic change. To demonstrate is to *show or prove something clearly and convincingly*. Demonstrating is behavioral. How does a leader demonstrate his commitment to the diversity and inclusion journey?

He lets the whole organization know and feel his commitment to making sure everyone has a voice and every voice is heard. "I constantly talk to and listen to people from all over the company and from outside regarding their thoughts on diversity and inclusion. I incorporate their ideas into the way I think about diversity. Our greatest asset is our people and their many ways of interpreting the world" (Tom Freston, Viacom).

Leaders in this discussion are people who have the power to set the standards of behavior because they have position, influence and the ability to reward or to punish. Phillip and Victor represent leaders and leadership styles.

IQ and EQ

It is clear that both **Phillip** and **Victor** are intelligent. They come from reputable universities, have graduate and post-graduate education and graduated at or near the top of their classes. They have mastered massive amounts of information, are extremely well read and articulate, and both men have solid communication skills. So the question is, what separates them, enabling one to lead in ways the other cannot?

Could it be emotional intelligence quotient (EQ)? If one of these two archetypal leaders has a higher emotional intelligence quotient than the other one, might it let him more quickly and easily create a diverse and inclusive environment?

In order to answer that question I researched the literature on EQ. John Mayer and Peter Salovey first formally defined the term 15 years ago. Their thesis was simple. "Our ability to engage in the highest levels of thought isn't limited to intellectual pursuits like calculus," Mayer contended. "It also includes reasoning and abstracting about feelings. And that means that among those people that we refer to as warmhearted or romantic or fuzzy – or whatever sometimes-demeaning expressions we use – there are some who are engaging in very, very sophisticated information processing. This type of reasoning is every bit as formal as that used in solving syllogisms."[xix]

Simply put, EQ is (depending on whether you use the originators – John Mayer, Peter Salovey – and later David Sluyter, the more famous David Goleman or the more moderate Steve Hein) the ability to develop skills that let one understand and interpret emotions related to oneself and others.

Whether EQ is more important or less important than intelligence quotient (IQ) – as measured by standardized exams like the SAT test and the *Simon-Binet Scale* – is debatable (and there are thousands of pages that do just that). What I found insightful and helpful in understanding why Phillip and Victor behave differently was the thesis that states, "We each experience countless interactions between intelligence and emotion, but only some of them make us smarter." This smaller subset of interactions – those that make us smarter represent what I refer to as emotional intelligence and this is what I will examine more closely. It is the notion that emotions sometimes enrich thought, leading to more inclusive behaviors.

There is an abundance of social science research showing that the experience of strong feelings may help us perceive fresh alternatives and make better choices. It may be the basis for the saying, "Necessity is the mother of invention." Emotional intelligence could make the difference between a conventional decision and a daring one, between a stilted speech and one that soars – or, in the psychologist's whimsical example, "between constructing the Brooklyn Bridge, with its renowned beauty, and the more mundane 59th Street Bridge."[xx] Dr. Martin Luther King Jr. and Golda Meir are two people who were great because they were both rational and emotional.

So how does EQ apply to our two leaders, Phillip and Victor, in their journey of long-term systemic change?

EQ is:

- The ability to perceive and identify emotions in faces, tone of voice, body language.

- The capacity for self-awareness of your feelings as they occur.

- The ability to incorporate feelings into analysis, reasoning, problem solving and decision-making.

- The ability to understand the potential of your feelings to guide you to what is important to think about.

Leaders on our journey need the competencies of self-awareness and the ability to incorporate feelings into the dialogue. Individual employees or members of groups may require you to call these skills into service at convenient or inopportune times.

Here's an example: Several members of your women's network are attending the regional State of the Company meeting. As the senior executive, you make sure part of your report covers the company's diversity efforts and successes. You are proud of the work the organization has done and have been waiting for an opportunity to share it. A female senior analyst asks, "Can you tell us why we've not seen more women promoted into senior leadership positions?" You answer her question with facts about the recruiting efforts and restate your commitment to increasing the presence of women in top positions. Another member of the women's network says, "With all due respect, I've heard this for several years, but there doesn't seem to be any change." Depending on whether you are Victor or Phillip you will respond differently to this exchange.

Victor responds by nodding in the woman's direction and asking for the next question. He has not mastered the ability to identify emotions in faces, tone of voice, and body language of others. He does not notice the women glancing at each other. He misses the look of disappointment on the face of the first and second questioners. He is confident he has answered the question on the floor with his first response. His behavior is a clear signal to the members of the audience that he is finished with this discussion and it is time (for the wise) to move on.

Victor's posture and response to the second questioner (ignoring someone is in fact a clear response) does not seem rude or inappropriate to him. He is confident that all is well. He is also unaware that his personal "hot button"[xxi] has been pushed. Even if he feels a twinge of anger, he can quickly dismiss it as unimportant in this discussion and *move on.*

Phillip responds by first acknowledging his frustration with the difficulties and challenges of changing the face of his staff. He is aware that the second question has pushed one of his buttons and that he is feeling slightly annoyed. He is also aware of the women's frustrations; he can see it on their faces and in their body language. He begins his response by sharing with the audience his challenges and struggles with increasing the visible diversity of women. He talks about what's worked and what's not netted them the desired results. Next, Phillip asks the women's network representatives to take an action item to develop ideas and sit with him to discuss them. He tells the group that if he does it alone everyone will become more frustrated and disappointed, but he believes together they will be able to achieve their shared goals. He finishes by acknowledging that this may seem to take longer than anyone would like, but he is convinced they will get it right. His final sentence is directed to the second questioner: "Did I answer your question?" She responds, "Yes, and thanks."

"All of the great leaders have had one characteristic in common: it was the willingness to confront unequivocally the major anxiety of their people in their time. This, and not much else, is the essence of leadership."
— John Kenneth Galbraith

Phillip's behaviors signal his commitment to inclusion and a willingness to continue the dialogue as long as needed for the organization to achieve its goals. He is clearly committed to long-term systemic change.

EQ is also:

- The ability to solve emotional problems, to identify and understand the relationship between emotions, thoughts and behavior and to see how thoughts can affect emotions or how emotions can affect thoughts.

- The ability to understand how emotions can lead to behaviors and to see the *value* of emotions.

- The ability to take responsibility for one's emotions and happiness, to turn negative emotions into "teachable moments"[xxii] (my words) and the ability to help others identify and benefit from their emotions.

One of the most powerful tools I use to help leaders develop their ability to understand the relationship between emotions and behaviors, to "get it," is the notion of privilege. Unveiling privilege, the "invisible weightless knapsack of special provisions, maps, passports, code books, visas, clothes, tools and blank checks"[xxiii] is a key to cultural competency and a necessity for great leaders.

Leaders and Privilege

When I was young and I would complain about what I did not have, my mother (who loved clichés) would say, "I cried because I had no shoes and then I met a man who had no feet." As a child that made as much sense as "eat, people are starving in India" (the fact that it was always some country of brown people was lost on me for many years). The idea that I was better off than someone else was never solace for whatever I felt was missing. This is a crucial point in the development of the leader.

The ability to have empathy and understand the relationship between emotions, thoughts and behaviors is enhanced by understanding *what I have*. The discussion that unearths *what I have* is an uncomfortable one to lead and participate in. The discomfort is usually around the emotion of guilt and will often appear as anger. "I've never had any privileges, and I don't appreciate being made to feel bad." Beneath the surface can be shame: "I don't like that the world is not as fair or accommodating for others and gives me unearned rights." The truth is, all of us have privilege.

My lesson:

I was conducting a workshop for LaMaxxe Inc. in Arizona. The executive sponsor was a double amputee. I found out that he and I were both going to New York City a few days after the workshop. I was staying at a hotel in the Financial District and asked where was he staying, hoping we could have lunch or dinner. When he told me he was staying at a "finer" hotel in midtown (the work was in the Financial District) I began to chastise him for not staying with the "peons." He calmly explained to me that the hotel I stayed at was not wheelchair user friendly (it met the letter of the law, but not the spirit). He then told me a story of an earlier visit when he stayed at the hotel where I was staying.

Here's his story (it's close to verbatim and it will stay with me forever):

"I was dressed in my suit and ready to go to the office. Although the building is only four blocks from the hotel, the sidewalks and roadway are difficult to impossible to navigate in my chair. I told the concierge I needed a taxi. The taxis line up outside the hotel hoping to get a fare to the airport, but they have to take you wherever you want to go. The cab pulled up, I got out of my wheelchair and into the cab. The doorman put my chair into the taxi trunk. He then leaned in and told the driver that I was going four blocks away. I could tell the driver was pissed, but he had to take me. When we got to the office building, I paid him (with a large tip for a four-block ride) and waited with the door open for him to bring my wheelchair from the trunk to the passenger door. The driver got out, threw my chair onto the sidewalk (still folded) and got back into the cab. He did not say anything or look at me; he just faced forward in silence. After a minute or two I realized he meant for me to get out. I had to crawl out of the cab, slide my briefcase on the sidewalk, set up my chair and retrieve my belongings. The driver sped off as soon as I got out the door. Although several people stopped to help me, it was one of the worst experiences I've had. From that day forward I stay at a hotel far enough away that the driver doesn't feel cheated and I don't risk that kind of humiliation."

I was mortified. I felt ashamed because I am able-bodied and clueless about the privileges that come with that "invisible, weightless knapsack," as Peggy McIntosh calls it. I felt guilty that I'd never thought past my worldview to look at the world through someone else's eyes. I was angry at the cab driver. I knew that this emotion was as useless as being angry with someone who yells a racial slur and drives off.

There were several things I could have done with my feelings of guilt and shame. I could have denied them. That would probably have led to remaining ignorant of my privilege and how it lets me do something about injustice. I used the tool of substitution (see Tools in chapter six) because it let me do what I advocate for others: face my emotions, own them and think about ways that my (able-bodied) status benefits me. Being conscious of privilege also lets me make the connection between thoughts, emotions and behaviors. Now I could begin the work to ensure that my status did not disadvantage others.

Understanding how I am advantaged is essential to my development as a leader. If I do not see my *privilege, I cannot help others to see theirs.*

It opens my eyes to the micro-inequities – the small indignities that mount up and over time create an exclusive and hostile workplace.

Seeing *what I have that others do not* lets me understand that others suffer from actions about which I am clueless.

It lets me address issues that I was previously unaware of. That is the work of leaders. When we identify and understand how feelings like guilt and shame, anger and joy influence our behaviors and how we see people; we can make systemic changes like insuring that our facilities are accessible for people with disabilities or that our promotion efforts include people of color.

Victor refuses to acknowledge his privilege, the unearned benefits he takes for granted. He is positive that everything he has is the result of his hard work. He is convinced that he does not have any 'advantages.' The result is he cannot think about how to change the ways the organization disadvantages those without his level of privilege.

Phillip embraces the discomfort of his unearned advantage. He can own it and recognize that the feelings of guilt and shame are normal. He can also develop strategies for the organization that will have long-lasting positive effects. A "Phillip" explained it this way, "One of the most difficult things I realized was that part of what I would have to do was give up some of my power and my privilege. More than just share it, I have to be willing to give some of it up. People don't do that voluntarily." Leadership is recognizing privilege and being willing to relinquish its benefits.

Remember, psychologists' research hypothesizes that the experience of *strong feelings* may help us perceive fresh alternatives, make better choices and, paradoxically, maintain an *even* emotional keel. Emotional intelligence could make the difference between a conservative choice and a bold one, between an unoriginal idea and a creative one. In these times of great competition, which do you choose?

Leaders Exhibit Courage

"If you cain't bear no crosses, you cain't wear no crown."
(African-American spiritual)

In order to make deep and lasting changes, leaders will have to make difficult decisions. Often in the early stages one of the toughest decisions a leader has to make is when he has clear evidence a senior staff member does not support the diversity and inclusion initiative. Here's how it happens: This CEO recognizes that one of his most influential and trusted staff members is sabotaging his efforts to create an inclusive culture. The person may be your plant manager, medical director or chief financial officer (CFO). The sabotage may be a show of nonsupport; at one town hall meeting a senior member was overheard telling several employees that he did not understand why his CEO was focused on this diversity crap and not on real business issues. Or perhaps the staff member consistently misses his diversity metrics – whether those are hiring, promotion or educational measurements. No amount of help and support from you or human resources and no amount of coaching improves the plant manager's performance. You've tried talking, yelling, threatening and listening. You begin to notice that the overt disobedience is contagious. The medical director's staff members start to fail to achieve their metrics, and then there are conversations about how it's just a "silly thing the CEO is pushing."

Victor makes excuses for his manager's behavior and points to his record in other important areas of the business where he has achieved and maybe exceeded his goals. What Victor doesn't say, but what is possibly true, is that this CFO is "one of the 'Victor's club' members" and Victor is very comfortable with him. After all, he is successful *because of* the CFO, and replacing him is risky and difficult.

Phillip realizes he is at an intersection. If he takes the personally easy road and ignores the director's behaviors, he sends a message that travels further than the corporate jet. Phillip takes the other path. He makes the tough and courageous decision to treat his executive's inability to achieve his inclusion and diversity goals in the same way he treats executives who do not achieve their sales or customer service goals – he takes action. One "Phillip" put it this way: "My management leadership group has to get it, and if there is someone who can't get it in a reasonable amount of time they need to go. In the past I let it go on much too long, and it cost the initiative a lot of time, energy and credibility."

"Time is neutral and does not change things. With courage and initiative, leaders change things."

(Jesse Jackson)

Sometimes courage is called for by circumstances. The organization is publicly embarrassed by a scandal or a class-action lawsuit. The *natural* tendency is to become more risk averse, to retreat to the familiar like tomato soup on a cold day or to view people as safe based on similarity or familiarity. Courageous leaders resist this.

This is the letter I sent to a group of leaders when the company faced one of the most difficult times in its history:

Dear Leaders,

Maslow theorized that when faced with concerns about basic needs (food, shelter and sex [hey, Maslow said it, not me]) or safety (financial or personal) human beings could not and would not focus on personal achievement or the inclusion or welfare of others. In this time of great challenge and opportunity where many people are feeling less than secure, leadership demands that we remain focused on those things we valued a week ago – inclusion, diversity, risk taking and creativity. It is our greatest challenge to avoid retreating to the safe and familiar – whether that is the diversity of employees we surround ourselves with or the ways we operate and make business deci-

sions. The leadership's unparalleled contribution to the long-term health of the company will be a spirit of greatness based on our diversity and our ability to do the improbable – and make it look easy.

Don't back away from our call to lead through this time of challenge – we're a great place to work, and you're great leaders!

The journey toward diversity and inclusion is a long and sometimes difficult one. For leaders it's more than attending a recruiting conference or addressing an employee network group. Somewhere between year one and year seven, there will be a very difficult decision to make – a decision that will signal the depth of your commitment.

Israel 2002. I was told I could talk about many dimensions of diversity, but could not talk about the Jewish/Arab issue. I understood the rationale – with daily suicide bombings killing employees and family members of employees, it wasn't a simple diversity issue. Throughout the two weeks of training, Jewish managers approached me and asked why we didn't talk about it (I think they meant why didn't I talk about it – as an outsider I have more latitude to touch the untouchable issues). I told them I had agreed as part of my coming to Israel to remain silent. I regret that now. I think one of the things we can do as leaders is always talk about the "elephant in the middle of the room" (the thing that everyone notices but pretends doesn't exist). It is possible that if we could have talked about the hardest issue, we would have had greater progress with the easier ones like gender and accommodations for orthodox Jews.

The lesson: Whatever you're not talking about is how the organization or the world keeps us separate. Even if we disagree, it's courageous to talk about the really tough issues. I met a Jewish woman whose husband was killed by a suicide bomber. She talked about having friends who were Arabs and who were afraid to speak up – to say that they did not hate Jews. She and I talked at length about how important it was for her to make sure her three children did not hate Arabs and Muslims - that they understood that a horrible person had committed an unthinkable crime, but that to hate a race or religious group was an unthinkable crime too. She was much more inclusive than most of her colleagues; maybe it's because she'd learned to act courageously and speak the truth.

"It seems to me that – at least in our scientific theories of behavior – we have failed to accept the simple fact that human relations are inherently fraught with difficulties and that to make them even relatively harmonious requires much patience and hard work."

– (Thomas Szasz, M.D.)

Leading requires courage. It mandates that we do things that are personally and professionally difficult.

Roger is a regional HR executive I met while working with a large consumer products company. He was asked to help his enthusiastic and committed company president lead the diversity initiative. When we began the work we talked about ensuring that the definition of diversity was fully inclusive. The organization's regional office was located in an area of the country known for religious conservatism that publicly denounced any orientation other than heterosexuality. Roger was an active and involved leader in the religious community.

Early in our relationship it became apparent that his directive to add sexual orientation to the definition – and to the support, development and retention efforts – made him uncomfortable. As a good soldier he was willing to say the right words, write the policy statements and provide leadership to the other executives. The problem was, he was uncomfortable with gay, lesbian and transgendered people. He knew he needed to resolve the conflict between what he felt his corporate position required and his religious values, family history and cultural foundation.

I suggested he pair up with Peter, a colleague who was openly gay. I suggested this pairing because they shared the same religious affiliation and grew up in the same city. I also knew that Peter needed to look at his biases and examine the prejudices he held about heterosexual members of his religious community. In a private meeting, Peter told me he viewed everyone affiliated with Roger's religion as "gay-hating religious zealots." When I pointed out that this was his religion also, he said it was different for him.

"We look at others through a magnifying glass and ourselves through rose-colored glasses."

(Joyce Meyers)

As part of an educational leadership experience I often ask participants to pair up with someone they view as "different", meet at least once a month for a year and explore diversity together. The only requirement is they meet regularly. They can discuss any topic, attend events or simply sit in silence. Roger agreed to the arrangement.

Roger and Peter, his "diversity partner," spent hours discussing their lives, beliefs and aspirations. Roger told me he wanted to understand why another person's sexual orientation made him uncomfortable. It was not enough to ascribe it to the way he'd been raised or even his religious beliefs – he was friends with ethnic minorities even though several members of his family were openly prejudiced and several of his male friends were Army veterans who had killed people in war, an act forbidden in his religion.

Roger and Peter exhibited courage. They were willing to sit with their discomfort and confront their prejudices. They did not shy away from difficult topics that sometimes made them angry or uncomfortable with one another. They saw themselves in the other person's negative examples of prejudice and intolerance. Their work paid off. Each man reported growing in his understanding of himself and learning to see the world through the eyes of a colleague. Roger reports years later that although it was painful to look at himself through Peter's eyes, it made him a better manager, leader and ultimately a better person. He and Peter maintain contact, although both have left the company.

The work of leading an organization on the inclusion and diversity journey requires patience, hard work and extraordinary commitment on the part of the leaders. Managing diversity with the complexities of biases, preconceived notions, cultural baggage and human differences and similarities creates potholes and sharp curves, steep climbs and surprising challenges along the way.

"There's a difference between interest and commitment. When you're interested in doing something, you do it only when it's convenient. When you're committed to something, you accept no excuses; only results."

(Ken Blanchard)

A serious commitment:

Airwelt's corporate headquarters is located in a small, White, ultra-conservative city in the Midwest. This city and several of the surrounding counties proudly share their reputation for fundamentalist Christian values and racial homogeneity.

Interestingly, Airwelt's founder was a staunch supporter of diversity and justice from the beginning, even though the company headquarters were located in an area of the U.S. that was not seen as liberal or progressive. The original founder established the company's civil rights reputation in the 1960s with his support of the NAACP[xxiv] and the work of Dr. Martin Luther King Jr.

In the mid '90s I worked with Airwelt's president before he was promoted to CEO. We were in year two of the journey and making steady progress. Shortly after his appointment, the CEO decided to approve same-sex health care benefits for the employees. He was advised by several members of his executive staff that this might not be a particularly smart thing to do as one of his early acts (this came shortly after President Bill Clinton had taken gay rights to the American public and taken a political if not personal pounding). To his critics and those who asked him not to do it, the CEO responded, "I think it's important for an organization to do things that are difficult, especially when it's the right thing for the employees and our culture."

The decision resulted in protests outside several of the company's facilities, personal threats that resulted in his needing police protection for himself and his family, and as he said, "seeing the really ugly side of human behaviors." It also changed the organization and galvanized many employees' commitment to the diversity and inclusion journey. Several national groups recognized the company for its leadership in granting same-sex benefits and its diversity initiative.

When I asked the CEO why he took this particular risk so early in his tenure he replied, "Instituting the health care benefits was something we should have done years ago. Additionally this ensured that everyone recognized that our leadership in this area was not just one of convenience, but rather one built on the principles of Dr. King."

This component of the commitment to long-term systemic change – the second of the $^7K^2S$ – is that leaders' behaviors mirror the changes they seek, that they *walk the talk*.

As Dr. Martin Luther King Jr. said, "The ultimate measure of a man is not where he stands in moments of comfort and convenience, but where he stands at times of challenge and controversy."

At some point in every leader's journey, there will come a time when you must do something difficult. It's just part of the journey. There's a mountain, or slippery path, a broken axle or a large boulder that must be moved. It will happen. The question for your leadership is: "How will we respond?"

Part of what makes the trip difficult is negative road signs that can lead to dead-end streets and closed highways.

Six Negative (Road) Signs:

1. "We need more data." A $192 million class-action settlement is only one data point, but seldom do we say "it's just a single data point. It's not enough." How much data do we need? Depends on where you sit. The assistant who feels excluded from the conversations and not allowed to contribute his ideas doesn't need additional data. The manager who witnesses the diverse team outperform her highest expectations doesn't need additional data. The manager who doesn't like the initiative and sees it as a waste of time will never have enough data.

2. "We want to measure everything." This is similar to "more data." Measure what's important to achieving the people and profit goals. Three things maximum. When you achieve one, add one.

3. "I can't hold her accountable for diversity." If you can hold managers accountable for customer service, service delivery, product quality, creative content or increasing market share, you can hold them accountable for diversity. All of these require management skills, e.g., communications, giving and receiving feedback, building teamwork and out-of-the box thinking.

4. "Too much on my plate to add diversity." You are always managing diversity and inclusion. You're doing it well or badly, but you're doing it. I can't put it on your plate; it's already there – even if you're hiding it like broccoli, trying to slide it onto the floor hoping the dog will eat it or hoping it will get so old and cold that you won't have to deal with it. My friends, it's right there on the plate, and it's not going anywhere.

5. "Two days is a lot of time! Our executives don't have two days for training." There are two ways to look at this statement. 1) "Well, how much time do you think the executives at the last three companies who were sued for over $48 million dollars spent before and after the lawsuits? I'd guess that two days looks pretty good to them." The problem with this approach is a) it's comparing apples (education on developing and evolving an inclusive culture) to pineapples (an EEO lawsuit that is the result of years of historical neglect). b) Most executives do not believe that their company is in any danger of being sued. There is no data that this can happen to them, and they feel that if this were a possibility they'd know about it in advance. c) You're asking me to put two days on my calendar in 2005 to avoid time I may have to spend in 2006. 2) A better answer. "Yes, two days is a lot of time. However, leaders at companies you compete with have found that setting the tone – walking the talk – cost much less than the cost of resistance, stopping and starting efforts, and external resources." Your leadership is what counts in diversity and inclusion as it does in all important cultural changes.

6. "We can't do this outside the U.S." The challenge of managing and leading people like me and people who are different from me is the same on every continent. The groups I view as "like and different" differ by geography, but the human elements of comfort, privilege and leadership are the same.

Tips for Leaders

- Conduct yourself with integrity. Don't tell a joke to your colleagues that you would not be comfortable telling in any setting.

- Think like a "minority." View the workplace from the perspective of the disabled or the gay employee. Is it accommodating and hospitable? If you have no idea, investigate.

- Establish a vision of what you want the organization to be, and measure all of actions against that vision. If the actions don't support the vision or are in conflict with it, ask yourself if it's worth it.

- Develop action plans that are goal-oriented. Review the goals and mini-goals regularly to see if you are on track. If you are not, evaluate your steps and adjust your plan accordingly.

- Get a coach — someone who is well regarded and whom you admire, someone who will tell you the truth. When you are faced with difficult situations, seek insight and advice or ask your coach to evaluate your decisions.

- Be willing to accept criticism. This will be most effective if you:

  1. Avoid being defensive. Be aware that EQ is the ability to identify and control your emotions.
  2. Treat the criticism as a "teachable moment" that has a short shelf life. Listen for the learning.
  3. Thank the person giving the criticism, even if you disagree with the content.

- Learn from your mistakes and missteps. There's nothing to gain from being defensive or blaming others.

- Develop your diversity and inclusion EQ. Part of the commitment is that you are seen as continuing to grow and learn. As John F. Kennedy said, "Leadership and learning are indispensable to each other."

The leader's commitment must be:

Visible. In every speech, message and communication, that is viewed as important. At LaMaxxe, Airwelt and StarrCom, employees *feel* the leader's commitment to the journey. Employees hear, witness and believe that their leader is committed to achieving diversity and inclusion and willing to stay the course through easy and difficult times. It is more than words and it is *in* the words.

Inclusive. The commitment has to be for all employees. The leader demonstrates this when she schedules meetings that share the burden and support on individuals who live close to *and* far from headquarters. The commitment has to be to develop all of the talent in the organization, not just a segment; to develop, engage and empower management and individual contributors, older and younger workers, technical and administrative talent.

Integrated. The leadership commitment has to be evident in policy formation and performance metrics — in the way the company does business and conducts meetings. It has to be threaded throughout all of the processes.

It must be apparent to everyone in the organization. Sometimes executives tell me it is impossible for them to make sure that everyone knows about their commitment to this work. My answer is: They already know about your commitment – and it may not be what you want them to think.

Chapter five

key #3 - support

Nusrat's Story

Working on the Diversity Council, as part of this incredible team, has been a profoundly moving and transforming experience. When I came on board, I knew I was signing up for an important and challenging task, but had no idea of the complexity of the issues involved or the level of commitment required.

A lot has been achieved in the past two and half years by the Diversity Council and by other initiatives within MTV Networks. A lot has also changed because of the turn of events that we could never have imagined.

When I joined the council, I had, in retrospect, the arrogant notion that I understood the issues around diversity because I am from a diverse background and have lived in countries where diversity is a fact of life. I thought I could be effective because I wasn't a stranger to the subtle cruelties of exclusion. I had imagined that creating an inclusive environment at MTVN was another management challenge, perhaps somewhat bigger than ones we had successfully overcome in the past, but certainly a goal that could be achieved fairly quickly.

I was wrong.

As my understanding of issues like race, religion, sexual orientation, etc. became more sophisticated, I realized we had undertaken a very complex task that would take years to accomplish and forever change us as individuals.

And so I've changed. I am more sensitive, more empathetic, more tuned to others' differences and similarities than ever before. I see the world from a very different perspective than previously. I feel richer and fuller, but I also feel sadder, more tempered and realistic than before.

We've all come a long way, and so has this organization that we love. But there is so much more to be done. I feel that our tenure has been just about laying the foundation and that the synagogues, temples,

*mosques and churches of diversity still need to be built upon this foun-
dation. Sometimes I feel like all our conversations and memos and
meetings about inclusivity are theoretical and the reality on the
ground, in the offices and cubicles where we work, has not changed.
But the days I feel like this are very few, and they are usually the days
when I've had a bad commute.*

*Because the truth is, things have changed, things are changing rap-
idly, and the results are tangible, visible and extremely gratifying.*

*I want to thank all of you for who you are and what you've taught
me. I am privileged to have come to know you and touched by your sin-
cerity and kindness and the hard work you have done. We have a
common thread, an invaluable, shared experience and a longing that
will always connect us.*

(Nusrat Durani, MTV Networks Council member)

The Supporting Cast

The leadership can set the vision, communicate the commitment to
the organization and establish the direction of the diversity and
inclusion journey, but it is impossible for one person to move the
wagon alone. Imagine three thousand employees standing on a
wagon (albeit a large one). No matter how strong or strong-willed,
determined and dedicated CEOs are, they cannot move the wagon.
They can set the direction the wagon will travel, the schedule of
events and make everyone aware of the expected outcomes, but
without help they cannot move the wagon one inch. They need help.
They need a village. This help comes from the individuals who agree
to provide strategic guidance and operational support to the leadership and the organization.

Who are these individuals, why do they do it and what help can
they provide? How is their work visible, inclusive and integrated?

Does This Sound Familiar?

An executive discusses her sincere desire to have a diverse and inclusive environment. She outlines the business case, the answer to
the question, "Why are we spending 1000 yen or ten minutes on
this?" She and her executive team develop the organization's diversity strategy, metrics and timetable. In various venues she talks

about diversity and inclusion. She is confident the organization is moving forward. She assumes everyone in the organization shares her view of the world.

One day a group of GLBT employees ask for time on her calendar. They share with her chronicles of abusive managers, excluding behaviors based on sexual orientation and jokes, e-mails and memos that could easily be used to document the legal definition of a hostile work environment. She is dismayed, surprised and angry. How could this be going on in *her* organization and why didn't she know about it? When she asks her senior team about the allegations, she gets responses that range from denial ("it's not true" and "it's a few people who are problems, blowing things up") to blank stares. I'm not sure which is more difficult, the blank stares or the "it wasn't me" leaders. For the executive, the journey becomes a bumpy, winding, narrow road. This challenge can occur in London, Kentucky or London, England. The group may be different, but the dilemma is similar. The distance between the leader's view of the diversity initiative and the employees' experience of the initiative is great.

Here's why:

At The Top – At the executive meeting there is a two-hour discussion with the senior staff and their management group to ensure that everyone has a clear picture of the future—with clearly defined roles, responsibilities and expectations. During this discussion there are slides with tables and graphs, handouts, data sheets and a list of deliverables with dates.

In The Middle — Managers spend twenty minutes at an already packed staff meeting discussing the "program." There is a one-page handout and two slides.

On The Floor — At this "discussion," managers and supervisors have too much on their plate already to add something else, especially something they are not clearly competent to discuss. The handout (which is three bulleted sentences) is left on the table at the back of the room. Most of the time, this is where the pulse of the initiative becomes weak and faint. It evolves from a vibrant and energizing discussion to the last item on a packed agenda to recycling.

The CEO decides to investigate the allegations from the GLBT group. She asks her executives to look into this issue and come back with data and recommendations. The information comes to her in spurts. Some of it points to glaring problems, but much of it is subtle. She needs help.

Her executives tell her they need help.

"Where do you learn how to pay attention to diversity without stereotyping? I'd like to find out what the issues in my group are, but I don't want the liability attached to it. I'm at a loss and have no idea where to go or even what I need."

Employees tell her they need help.

"My manager doesn't have a clue about managing diversity. She says she supports it, and in the same breath she tells a joke making fun of one of the gay employees. Her boss thinks she's on board, so what can I do?"

Who and where are the individuals who will provide the help, the strategic and operational support? The answer is they are *everywhere*. They are in the executive offices, middle-management cubicles, shop floor stations and driving to customer sites. Some are members of minority communities, and others represent the majority. The executive needs a plan to enlist these allies.

Executive Diversity & Inclusion Council (EDIC)

For many organizations the Executive Diversity & Inclusion Council is the initial level of support. Organizations use various titles, e.g., Executive Inclusion Council, Corporate Diversity Council and Executive Council on Diversity. The work is essentially the same: to provide strategic direction and help. The "best in class" executive diversity councils are led by the CEO or president and have high-level decision makers such as the HR executive, two to three direct reports to the CEO and other senior personnel from throughout the organization. The CEO's presence and leadership are critical to the success of the initiative and a cornerstone of its progress and success. It reinforces the other leaders' commitment to the effort.

Most of us know that having executive involvement and support is usually the key factor in any successful business undertaking. It sets the tone and shapes the standards of behavior throughout the organization. The presence of an Executive Council sends a clear message that diversity is important.

A second equally critical benefit (although not always apparent) is that the top-level executive learns skills that are valuable in today's global economy. We see that when executives spend time each quarter having dialogue about how to make diversity and inclusion work, they learn to clearly articulate and communicate the links between diversity and business success.

As they learn to recognize the complexities of sustaining an inclusive and diverse culture, they begin to see and appreciate the impact of the organization's policies and practices on an increasingly multicultural and global workforce. They learn to integrate diversity into everyday events such as recruiting and retaining their talented, diverse workforce.

Executive Diversity & Inclusion Councils (EDICs) serve several purposes.

As I often say, "Innovative, creative and inspired responses to challenges and opportunities in the workplace and the marketplace flow largely from the associations and connections we make between the problem at hand and the knowledge and experiences we hold in our head."

EDIC members provide different interpretations of the culture, opportunities and challenges. They view the corporate diversity and inclusion dilemmas from different disciplines, with individual backgrounds and histories and multiple cultural realities. Because they represent a spectrum of views, they provide the leader with fresh and diverse perspectives and solutions. Members of the council often have different networks to go to for ideas and information. Some of the EDIC members may have more insight into the issues being raised because they have conducted surveys or polled focus groups. On the council will be varying levels of cultural competency (see Chapter six for more on cultural competency levels).

The EDIC:

One of the first tasks for the council is connecting the issues in the current environment, the desired outcomes and the business case. It is as David Cottrell says in his book "Monday Morning Leadership": It's important to "keep the main thing the main thing." If the main thing is to attract and retain a talented and diverse workforce, sustain an inclusive culture and environment, and continuously grow people and profits, then that is what the council focuses on accomplishing. All inquiry, effort and measurements are connected to this simple fact.

The EDIC may take responsibility for fully developing the business case. The business case discussion (in chapter three) is an example of an Executive Council driven effort. In that example the council, with help from a cross section of employees, identified the components of the business case. The council was responsible for reinforcing the importance of the business case with the executives and management staffs. The work an EDIC does to provide direction for the leadership serves also as a development activity for council members.

The council, however powerful and directed they are, cannot single-handedly provide the strategic and operational help needed. On the journey toward diversity and inclusion, the work has to touch many more employees. Executives and the EDIC can define the vision and direction, but they need additional leaders to align and motivate people.

To do this, other resources are needed. Many organizations find strategic support in the form of general Diversity Councils, sometimes known as Regional Councils or Local Councils. These councils are made up of a wider selection from the organization than the Executive Council.

Their work includes:

- Driving diversity into the business units.
- Helping the organization reach representation goals.
- Monitoring representation at senior levels.
- Sponsoring educational events.
- Increasing supplier diversity representation.
- Establishing accountability and measurement procedures.
- Supporting the work of the executive council.

Networks/Affiliation Groups

Another piece of the operational support comes from employee networks or affinity groups. Best practices companies have between three and thirty networks and affinity groups — people joined by a set of common characteristics, such as race, gender, sexual orientation, religion or physical disability.

Their charter includes:

- Identifying areas in need of support and attention.
- Providing feedback to executives and councils.
- Giving social and business support for members.

- Aiding multicultural marketing efforts.
- Improving employee feedback.
- Opening new markets.
- Linking with community and national organizations.
- Improving the work environment.

Networks function most effectively when they have clearly defined roles, objectives, structure, a relationship to leadership, and executive support.

Networks, councils and affinity groups are ideal ways for the initiative to be visible and inclusive. These support structures offer numerous opportunities for the organization to showcase the initiative and garner assistance from a large part of the employee population.

Executive Diversity Leaders

A missing piece has been knowledgeable internal leadership -- senior level individuals who can provide more than leadership; are skilled facilitators and problem solvers. Here's the question:

Who's leading tomorrow?

Your CEO is committed to the success of the diversity initiative, a champion and its most ardent supporter. Your organization has an Executive Diversity and Inclusion Council and several funded and resourced affinity groups. Sounds wonderful, doesn't it? Well, what happens when the CEO leaves or when the focus on diversity is replaced by the need to avert a hostile takeover? Furthermore, how confident are you that the individuals who are leading the effort now and in the future have a solid diversity education and the initiative's design, direction and metrics are based on sound diversity principles? How do you ensure that the next generation of leaders are culturally competent, knowledgeable and prepared to continue the journey toward inclusion and diversity?

The important quality for a diversity/inclusion leader is the ability to motivate others to be a part of the leadership, and see it as a part of their personal day-to-day performance. [To] be able to draw others into the debate and be the catalyst who can convince others that helping to change the content and character of the workplace makes the organization better.

(Ted Childs, IBM)

My answer – the Executive Diversity Leaders Development Program (EDLDP).

It addresses these challenges: loss of momentum that results from change in leadership or focus and the need for formally trained and educated leaders.

WHO

Select eight to ten senior level managers from around the globe to participate in a twenty-month assignment.

High-potential executives.

These are the executives who are sitting at the senior table or will be in the near future. They are leading key areas the organization depends on for future growth. They come from every part of the organization. In a health care organization they can be the medical director or director of Community Medical Services. In manufacturing it's often a plant manager or the purchasing manager. The selected individual may be the executive vice president of marketing or VP of new products. Notice I intentionally omitted the executives from human resources and legal. These two functions provide significant support to these executives.

With solid management skills.

This is not a program to develop poor managers. (Although managers at this level *should* be skilled, that is not always the reality.) These leaders will need a solid understanding of management principles, including communications, giving and receiving feedback, negotiating and conflict resolution.

Willing to learn.

There is a great deal of information they will need to master. They will be asked to read significant amounts of the current literature, attend events, watch videos and engage in discussion to increase their understanding and cram four years of education into eight months.

Courageously introspective.

It is imperative that each leader selected is willing to look at himself or herself in the mirror. Each EDLDP participant will identify those things that interfere with creating a diverse and inclusive environment. He/she will be asked to identify personal biases and prejudices and develop ways to address them. In order to help others address their prejudices, this individual will need to understand how to overcome their own biases.

Additional skills:

- Effective coaches who base the coaching relationship on trust, not similarity.
- Optimistic about human nature and believe that people want to be inclusive.
- Able to meet people where they are — and not where I want them to be.
- Can give people opportunities to take risks and learn from their mistakes.
- Listen more than they talk.
- Patient, and are willing to find the "coachable" and teachable moment.
- Speak candidly, but dispense their message in the right-size dosage.
- …willing to be personally accountable and take ownership for behaviors.
- Approach resistance and reluctance to change with curiosity.
- Aware of their own strengths and limitations.

What is the EDLDP?

Phase One is designed to provide the participants with three to five years of industry knowledge in eight months. This is ambitious, but doable. This phase is a combined academic and on-the-job formal education program. This curriculum mirrors other executive development programs. There are case studies and significant reading requirements – eight to twelve text books, including "Designing a House for Diversity" by Dr. Roosevelt Thomas, "A Peacock in the Land of Penguins" by Hateley Schmidt & Weiss, "The Diversity Dilemma" by Dr. Robert Hayles and "Measuring Diversity Results" by Edward E. Hubbard, plus stacks of articles, reference materials, including 2002 and 2003 WOW Facts, and online educational tools, e.g., The Diversity Channel and Diversity Inc.

Phase Two is a twelve-month assignment in which the participant has a dual role and title, e.g., vice president of programming and diversity leader (DL). He/she retains 75-85% of pre-program job responsibilities and acquires 15-25% new responsibilities for providing diversity expertise, leadership, coaching and direction to a designated part of the organization. The participants report to their line manager and the chief diversity officer (or other senior knowledge expert). Their performance review, bonus and other compensation are based on meeting established goals and metrics in both areas. Throughout this period the diversity leaders are continuously meeting with experts in the field of diversity to gain insights, address concerns, develop innovative ways to lead and maintain their sanity.

The Organization's Commitment

Before undertaking an endeavor of this magnitude an organization must recognize that the EDLDP requires major financial and managerial investment. Successful leaders (a criterion for inclusion in the program) are generally working at greater than 100% capacity. The organization has to examine the DL's workload in light of additional responsibilities, may need to fund temporary head count for the twelve-month period, shift current responsibilities or share an important talent resource with other parts of the company.

The Reward

The organization will end up with senior executives and leaders who understand what it takes to create and sustain a diverse and inclusive culture. They can be called on to provide leadership, support and champion new ideas, can coach, teach, develop strategy and provide direction to managers and supervisors while reducing the dependence on external training and consulting.

An eight-hour course stays with a manager for between two days and two weeks. As one DL stated, "This experience stays with you forever!"

Another leader described it this way: "It's like the yellow Volkswagen phenomena. Before you buy one, you never see one, but after you buy one, you see fifteen of them. Now everywhere I look I see diversity — on TV, on the covers of magazines in the checkout line and on the front page of The Wall Street Journal. I know it was always there, but I just didn't notice it."

These executives will continue to learn and grow, explore this topic and develop future best practices because their knowledge was built from the inside out (discovered by them), rather than the outside in (told to them).

The recipe:

- Begin with executive buy-in.
- Carefully select and mix in eight to ten high-potential executives.
- Marinate for eight months in intense education.
- Add clear deliverables.
- Generously top with daily challenges.
- Serve to the organization while still warm and fresh.
- Praise lavishly.

Chief Diversity Officer

The final piece of the puzzle is the chief diversity officer (CDO). The first question is, "Do we need one?" (You will definitely need human resources support and may need a program administrator who can report to EEO or legal.)

"No" if:

> You're in the Stage One of the journey (see chapter nine).
> You do not have executive-level authority – this position like the CFO and chief operating officer (COO) reports to the CEO.
> You want one because Jorge at ABC Company has one.
> You need someone to go to all those diversity events.
> You want someone to take care of this diversity stuff, e.g., developing training and scheduling council meetings.

"Yes" if:

> The executive and the leadership have set the tone and direction of the initiative.
> The organization is in Stage Two and especially if you're in Stage Three.
> You are ready for someone to identify the next level of achievement and help design the route to get there.
> You have a lot of money that you want to give to me. (Just checking to see if you're paying attention.)

Chapter SIX

learning

Training vs. Education

I wanted to learn French. I was scheduled to make a trip to Paris, and I'd heard they appreciated effort. I bought a cassette tape series (yes, it was that long ago), put it in my car deck and for several weeks a gentleman on the tapes and I conversed. He would speak and I would respond. It was perfect. I could tell him that I was hungry and wanted to eat now. We greeted each other and introduced Mr. Green to Miss Smith. I could get a pencil and ask someone to close the door. Somewhere between Boston and Paris (perhaps over the Bermuda Triangle) I lost my French. When I arrived in Paris, no one spoke the French that Mr. Tape and I spoke. I realized that the training I received was very different from the education I needed.

To change our organizations we must provide multiple, multi-layered training and educational opportunities.

> *Training (awareness and skills).*
> *Education (constant, broad, organization- and individually focused).*
> *Opportunities (passive, active, internal and external).*

"More than 95% of all Fortune 500 companies have engaged in some form of diversity training." (Functional Diversity Primer)

Training is by definition limited. To train is to "form by instruction, discipline, or drill," according to the Merriam-Webster dictionary. Training is too simple, and the workplace is too complex. This discipline requires building and developing skills while living inside a kaleidoscope with its constantly changing and fluid landscape.

Training can prepare me to begin the journey, but by itself it will have limited success. The tapes can teach me how to say *bonjour,* but they do not prepare me for the challenges of understanding what the baggage claim manager at the airport is saying about my lost luggage.

Awareness Training

I remember early in my career at DEC I was asked by a senior manager to provide a four-hour diversity awareness-training program for 135 employees. Many of my colleagues had diplomatically refused, but I was new on the job, young and, well, stupid. I quickly discovered the major problem with "training." At the end of the four hours we had "done" things. During one exercise, people experienced being in majority and minority groups. For the participants who spent their lives as members of the majority, the minority experience was humorously uncomfortable and brief. In the training, 136 people (me included) learned that diversity was an inclusive term and not code for affirmative action. I'm not sure what else we learned. I know we spent the full four hours together and that at the end I received great reviews, but I don't think the training accomplished what the organization needed: changes in head, hands and hearts; knowledge, skills and attitudes.

Not only is training limited, but also the path most organizations take to diversity and inclusion training is dubious.

The three most common ways organizations arrive at awareness training are:

One — You purchase an off-the-shelf product based on recommendations, colorful brochures with exciting and slick presentations, or you Google® with any of 50 key phrases that contain words like diversity training, cultural, multicultural education or anti-racism education, and the search will yield hundreds of companies offering a variety of products and services. Maybe you ask for recommendations from employees. They furnish you with contacts from past training experiences or individuals they know or have heard good things about.

The Pros: This method is quick and easy. With little or no effort it will generate an assortment of possibilities that can be presented to the organization. With thousands of possible firms and products, it is easy to find one that fits your organization's culture and needs. When you use the employee referral method, you further increase the possibility that the service delivery team you choose will be a fit for at least some part of the organization. Additionally, recommendations from internal sources build employees' investment in the success of the training and provide a network of supporters.

The Cons: It is difficult to impossible to determine if a seller is truly a "fit" for your organization. Fit is an elusive notion, for just as some coaches are better suited for certain teams, such as Phil Jackson for the Chicago Bulls and the Los Angeles Lakers, some courses are better suited for engineering organizations than for entertainment companies. Many times the employee's understanding of what the group needs differs widely from the views of the leaders. The recommendations are only as reliable as the recommenders.

Two — You purchase training packages that come with an external trainer. Many of the conferences that tout diversity education for human resources and diversity professionals are really opportunities for training providers to demonstrate their products and make sales presentations. Individuals return to their home organizations with business cards and good to great ninety-minute presentations.

The Pros: The recommender has witnessed some of the trainer's skills and may have some insight into her/his training style. It is possible to get information from others who have used this particular trainer or consulting firm and weigh the pros and cons of their feedback.

The Cons: Ninety minutes is not enough time to adequately judge a trainer's skills or to seriously test her knowledge of the subject. The other dilemma is that at conference workshops you will seldom see the types of resistance we know exist in our home organizations (after all, people paid to be in the room).

Buyers beware: When asked, "Is this training course customized?" everyone says, "Absolutely!" Now I'm not trying to get anyone in trouble or talk out of school as my mom would say, but if I were you I'd ask myself, "How is it possible to customize a course with little or no information (a maximum of sixteen hours of interviews, and discussions) about the company's culture, values, processes and unwritten rules?"

Three – You ask internal resources, trainers, HR consultants and HR managers to design and deliver the training. This one, at least at first glance, may appear most cost effective. The organization is confident that a skilled trainer who understands the culture of the group will be able to deliver training that matches the needs.

The Pros: This group knows and understands the workings of the organization – its values, foibles, myths and style. These facilitators know the group's weaknesses and strengths and there is a natural "fit" that makes it easier to align the training to the organization. The trainer(s) is generally comfortable delivering soft skills training to resistant and accepting participants.

The Cons: Unfortunately, if you are the internal resource being asked to develop the training, you are being asked to design "something" based on what you learned "somewhere." The organization effectiveness consultant or recruiter who delivered the course on conducting legally compliant interviews may not be knowledgeable or skilled in this particular discipline. She often reports difficulty addressing inappropriate behaviors and attitudes with individuals in the organization who are higher up the management chain. The consultant may also experience difficulty being heard and respected, for "a prophet in his own country" is often less valued.

Designing a Course

If your organization chooses option three and you want to develop your company's diversity awareness training course. Here's what it takes:

A Clear Definition and Direction

Awareness training has to focus on enabling employees to work more effectively with their increasingly more diverse teammates. It is important that this training provides participants with a definition of diversity that is inclusive.

This must be more than words; the training has to model the inclusivity of the definition. If the examples the trainer uses are primarily race based, if the training supports only a single learning style whether that's experiential or visual or if there is no room for dissention and disagreement, the participants will leave with an exclusive rather than an inclusive definition of diversity. The awareness training session should provide clear, easily understood definitions for commonly used terminology such as biases, stereotypes and inclusion.

An important element is an understanding of the business case for diversity. This reinforces the notion that awareness of diversity and inclusivity issues are a requirement of the job, a part of what employees are expected to know. The session should contain fun and useful learning experiences – participants are often apprehensive about attending diversity-labeled training, and it's important for them to have some fun and learn at the same time.

Lastly, the awareness training should provide practical tools that employees can immediately and effortlessly implement on the job.

Exceptional facilitation skills: A facilitator is "someone who aids or assists in a process, especially by encouraging people to find their own solutions to problems or tasks." I intentionally didn't say training skills because unlike accounting where there is information you want transferred and replicated, diversity awareness training courses are directed conversations that help people uncover and discover themselves. This is not a course with objective and immutable answers; it is a time for fluid ideas mixed with cultural ideology and individual histories.

Systems thinking ability: It is key that you view the course as part of a larger systemic change. It is not an event held on Tuesday in conference room 200; it is a part of the changing relationships between people and organizational processes. Systems thinking "focuses on how the thing being studied interacts with the other constituents of the system"[xxv]. In this case, diversity training looks at how individual biases, beliefs and cultures interact with organizational culture, values and goals. Systems thinking is essential because the diversity and inclusion journey is complex, old solutions that haven't worked probably won't and the solution is not obvious because it is *in the audience.*

More knowledge than your participants: It is not necessary to have twenty years of experience leading diversity and inclusion conversations, but it is important that you know more than the folks in the classroom. Here are the *must knows*:

- A working definition of diversity and inclusion that matches the organization's vision. The definition has to be as broad as your workforce and marketplace or customer base.
- An understanding of how biases - positive or negative preferences based on values, beliefs and prejudices influence our feelings of comfort or discomfort, our beliefs about ourselves and others and our working relationships.

- Understanding the difference between Affirmative Action, Valuing Differences and Managing Diversity. Affirmative Action is a proactive effort to make the workforce population resemble the external labor market[xxvi]. Valuing Differences is the personal work of identifying and addressing my biases, stereotypes and unexamined assumptions and appreciating the differences of age, gender, race, culture, physical abilities, sexual orientation and lifestyles. Managing Diversity is "a comprehensive managerial process for developing an environment that works for all employees."[xxvii]

- An intimate understanding of what privilege is and how it impacts people and practices. It is important to be comfortable describing how you have benefited from privilege, e.g., heterosexual, able-bodied or racial privilege. Be aware that privilege is one of the more difficult topics in diversity discussions.

Hudspa, cohones, guts, and nerve: On my business card my title is "CEO and Fearless Leader." Facilitating a class of twenty-five energetic (or worse yet, apathetic) individuals requires us to lead through our fears. You will need resolve, determination and willpower.

The first three can be learned. Attend courses and take notes on what worked for you and what you would change. Read books and articles, especially the diversity classics by Dr. R. Roosevelt Thomas, Judith Katz and Dr. David Thomas. Engage friends or colleagues in discussions that are interesting but not necessarily comfortable. The fourth requires taking a quantum leap of faith.

The real problem may not be how we decide what training to deliver and/or who will deliver it. The significantly more difficult challenge is what I call:

GO ... SET ... READY!

In the GO stage, someone decides, "We need diversity training." Human Resource sends out an email: Mandatory Diversity Training! Sign up now! The reasons are a varied as the organizations. Often it is caused by concern voiced by members of an affinity group. It may be based on a recommendation from a new employee. Or perhaps management is looking for a way to develop a culture of tolerance or inclusion.

Executives and other senior level employees — this includes the CEO and her/his staff — rarely receive truly meaningful training or education. More commonly they participate in what today's organizations call an "executive briefing" (fifteen to ninety minutes). The assumption is that today's executives have little time for anything more than this – the 10,000-foot view and only the really important data. "Just the facts, Ma'am."

As for the rest of the organization, the training focus is usually on getting the biggest return for the money. The message is "get as many people as possible *through* the diversity training in the shortest time possible," rather like a mandatory inoculation or as I sometimes think of it: "flea dipping" — a process designed to help fix an immediate problem, but without proper care and follow-up. So the "fleas" reappear in a few days.

When the focus of delivering diversity training is more on "numbers and speed," three things can happen:

1) Employees, especially "minorities", begin to ask questions (of managers and supervisors who don't have answers) about when and how the organization will respond to real or perceived problems.
2) Managers and supervisors, often ill at ease and unprepared to deal with these new "multicultural issues" and unsure how to proceed, can become overwhelmed.
3) There is a backlash from employees who don't understand why they "had to go" when it seems to them that everything was going well before the training.

By the time we discover that our managers are unprepared, the training has opened up wounds that heal slowly and the peace and tranquility we hoped for is a distant memory, it's too late. We've spent all of our money and come home to find we bought slacks too small and shoes three sizes too big. We have something, but it's not close to what we envisioned many months and thousands of dollars ago.

READY

The stage, which prepares the training for the organization and the organization for the training, never happened.

SET

The stage, which should happen after a pilot training session, was ignored.

Another try – READY, SET, GO.

READY

- Assess the culture. What do we want to change or address and why? What issues, challenges, gaps or needs is the training going to address? How will it improve our environment or help us achieve our goals?
- What worked in the past? Many times an organization has an initiative that was successful and can serve as a template. Identify what elements made it successful and replicate as many as possible. In the Niontek example, the Safety First Initiative (SFI) provided an exceptional example for the diversity and inclusion initiative.
- Communicate, communicate, and communicate. Remember, in order for the $^7K^2S$ to work they must be visible. Tell people what you're going to tell them (and why), tell them and then tell them what you told them. Diversity awareness training should not come as a surprise. When employees lack data they fabricate it. In the face of silence, they will fill in the gaps.

SET

- Develop the training outcomes with input from a diverse audience. Individuals will have different views of what is important and needed. This will help develop an effective program.

- Ensure that the trainer is more skilled and knowledgeable than the audience. Talk to others who have used this person. I know that everyone has to start somewhere, but how many of us want our organization to be on the plane that is the pilot's *first* flight? Check references with companies that are at a similar point in the journey as your organization.

- Check the design to make certain it has a high probability of accomplishing your goals. If you want people to have an expanded definition of diversity, check to make sure the examples the training uses are not predominately about race and/or gender, but are examples based on a broader definition, e.g., age, leadership style, communication patterns and sexual orientation.

- Communicate, communicate, and communicate.

GO

- Leaders first. If the organizational model is for leaders to lead and others to follow — if that's how the budgetary process is done or it's the way the business direction is established — then mirror this design.

- Fully engage leaders first. If it takes eight hours for employees to understand the work, it takes the same amount of time (or more) for leaders. There is no awareness that comes with a title. Money and power, yes; understanding how prejudice influences behaviors, no.

- Deliver the training with a two-to-three minute opening from a leader who has been through the program.

Best practices – the CEO makes a two-minute video about the training: why the organization is doing it, what she learned when she went through it, what she wants you to learn and her expectations for the future – after the training. A senior manager introduces each and every training session and sets the stage.

Looking at the big picture, understanding the need for a long-term commitment, the "Ready, Set, Go" solution not only gets you to the finish line first, but also helps you remain a winner.

Education Is The Key

Well, if training won't get us there, what will? Education.

In organizations we offer training, when it's education that employees need. An associate offered up this question when asked to define the difference between training and education, "Do you want your thirteen-year-old daughter/son to have sex training or sex education"? Even if you said neither, whenever I use this example of the difference between training and education, everyone chooses education!

Education is more than "instruction, discipline or drill." It has breath and depth. It is "[developing] mentally, morally or aesthetically: to provide with information or to persuade or condition to feel, believe or act in a desired way"[xxviii].

Education provides information that can shape what we know and how we behave. It can provide us with skills and will — experiences and information.

The key is not training, it is learning and educational opportunities that are available for all employees; customized and general enough to cover the breath of topics and integrated into the fabric of the organization.

Learning and educational opportunities — whether in the classroom, online, formal or informal, self-paced or facilitator-led, academic or experiential, skills-based or value-based — must focus on knowledge, skills and attitudes, or the head, hands and heart. The desired outcomes on the part of the funding or supporting organization and the individual are the same: that individuals become more knowledgeable – they have new and/or better-developed ideas about themselves and others. Education builds skills to address the challenges that come with working in and leading a diverse workforce and establishing an inclusive culture.

Education is key to the success of the diversity and inclusion journey because it fills the head with information, teaches the hands to act in a desired way and opens the heart to feel or believe in a desired way.

Education must focus on:

Developing Multicultural Competencies – looking at the culture of the organization and understanding the impact that has on its people.

Providing Tools – ideas, activities and solutions that management can use in the middle of the daily insanity.

Providing Experiences – they're much more powerful than an article or a lecture to help me understand a concept.

Developing Multicultural Competencies

Awareness and sensitivity training may provide information for the head, but not the skills needed to handle the tasks involved in working in and managing a diverse workforce. Developing cultural competencies — the behaviors, attitudes and practices the organization expects each person to demonstrate in their interactions with colleagues, customers and clients — addresses the hands, the skills and behaviors.

For managers, team leaders and supervisors, multicultural competencies include identifying the ways that individuals and groups are advantaged and disadvantaged by the organization culture.

Multicultural competencies ensure that management understands the link between an organization's successes and how well it utilizes its employee talent.

"It looks at the culture of the organization and how it manages people, its assumptions about development, and how it then either facilitates or inhibits the negative dynamics around diversity in the organization." (Robert Hayles)

For all employees it means behaviors and attitudes that transform knowledge about groups and cultures into workplace results. Cultural competency means that a person (1) learns to recognize and reject his or her pre-existing beliefs about a culture, (2) focuses on understanding information provided by individuals within the context at hand and (3) foregoes the temptation to classify or label people with cultural names. Cultural competence is a process that promotes the development of skills, beliefs and attitudes so we can accept and value others even when we may disagree with them[xxix].

Stage One — Denial[xxx]

Milton Bennett, who authored the "Developmental Model of Intercultural Sensitivity," describes six stages of development leading to cultural competency.

The first stage is *Denial*. Organizations and individuals at this stage deliberately pay no attention to cultural differences. This stage is the most negative end of the continuum. Individuals and groups refuse to recognize the presence or importance of cultural differences. In the denial stage, says Bennett, "not only are cultural differences not acknowledged, but [at the organization level] any perceived or real [deviances] from dominant mainstream culture are punished and suppressed."

Facilitating Change

There is little that can be done with the organization at this stage of the continuum. This is the "my way or the highway" mode of operating; unless and until something significant happens, the organization will not change. The good news is that few if any of these dinosaurs are left.

Stage Two – Defense

At this stage employees and organizations *choose to ignore* differences – to defend themselves by putting up a wall and refusing to see differences. At the same time the culture has established acceptable cultural behaviors, norms and values. Any departure from these established norms, from the notion of what is right and good, is viewed as bad and negative.

The Cornrow Incident

In the mid-'80s, I was invited to help a small (very profitable) manufacturing organization located in Pennsylvania "fix" a personnel problem. The plant population was 95.5% White and 4% Black. Prior to this conflict, the organization *chose,* perhaps unconsciously, to ignore the differences between Black and White employees. There were no courses, no dialogue or discussions that focused on acknowledging or addressing the differences and similarities between these two races. On the surface it appeared there were no differences. This façade was shattered when the only African-American saleswoman, Janet, came into the office with her hair in cornrows. People around her discussed her hair. White colleagues wanted to know if she was making a cultural statement. "I wasn't sure whether she was trying to say, 'Look at me, I'm Black and not like you' or 'I'm African and you need to understand that,' " said William, one of her co-workers.

There were memos, meetings and conference calls to determine what to "do about it." Her manager was worried that in her contact with customers, she might offend or make them uncomfortable. "I don't know how our clients will feel about that style," the manager said. "Personally I don't have a problem with it, but she probably should have warned me beforehand."

When I spoke with Janet about it, she was surprised to find out that anyone cared about her "new look". She said no one had mentioned or paid attention to any of her other hairstyles. Was her hair a statement or commentary on her ethnicity? No one asked her. But Janet's decision to braid her hair resulted in negative consequences, including personal ridicule and threats of dismissal. The *Denial* behaviors resulted in lost productivity: race and the "right kind of hairstyles" replaced customer service as the most commonly discussed topic for months. Several of the African Americans left the company. The $45 hairstyle cost the company thousands.

Facilitating Change

At this stage an organization is ready to be introduced to cultural differences and the influence they have on behaviors, attitudes, mores and values. There are numerous exercises that assist development from Stage Two to Three. Here are two exercises that introduce culture and meaning in non-threatening and interesting ways:

1. *Place a map of the world on a wall. Ask members of the group to place a red pushpin where they were born, a blue pin where their parents were born and a green one where their grandparents were born. (Be prepared for individuals who do not have this information.) After the pins are in place, ask people to share a couple of things from their history that make them a good employee.*

2. *Once a quarter, have a cultural lunch. Ask each person to bring a dish or a recipe from their culture with some information about how the dish is/was significant. For example, greens are significant to African Americans because during slavery they were a food source that would grow anywhere with little or no effort. Greens were nutritious, tasty and could be eaten alone or with lots of other foods.*

Stage Three — Minimization

The third stage is *Minimization* or *Cultural Blindness*[xxxi]. This is where most organizations in the 21st century begin their journey toward inclusion and diversity. They start with the belief that differences make no difference and that the important fact is we are all members of the human race. They are *culturally blind*. They believe that what works for the majority works for everyone.

At this stage employees and the organization see themselves as color blind or neutral toward diversity. There is an awareness of cultural, ethnic, gender, racial and style differences, but the party line is that "the only difference that counts is green." For many people this feels like a positive step. Neutral is so much better than the negative responses in Stages One and Two. The importance and significance of diversity is minimized and this is reinforced by practices and policies. Minorities and management alike may embrace this stage. It serves several purposes for both. For minorities it is evidence that whatever happens is the result of personal effort and not preferential treatment. For management it is proof that our decisions are based on objective criteria and not influenced by characteristics such as race and gender.

If, for example, a woman receives a promotion, at this stage of multicultural competency development everyone (overtly) agrees that she received it based on her personal merit and that no other factors influenced the decision. Everyone feels good about the outcome (her promotion) and the processes that led up to it (fair and equitable)

The Surround Factor

The problem with the minimization stage is that it ignores the "surrounding" factors. These factors are unwritten, unspoken, but powerful and influential attitudes and behaviors that "push and pull the cream to the top," as Roosevelt Thomas describes it.

Let's examine a typical promotion decision. Is it the "most qualified person" who gets it, or are there other factors involved in the final selection?

I believe that if we look closely at the promotion decision, we will see at least three *surrounding factors*. First, there is the *similarity/attraction* theory.

As I was doing research I found 320 pages dedicated to describing, elaborating on, expanding and disputing the similarity/attraction theory

— work begun in the early '60s by Donn Byrne. Those 320 (small academic print) pages tell us what many of us already know; people (that includes you and I) like, trust and are more comfortable with people who are similar, and dislike, distrust and are less comfortable with people who are "different."

Research studies have indicated that the more similar someone is to another person, the more he/she will tend to like that person (Buss, 1985; Davis, 1985; and Rubin, 1973). This 'liking' translates into positive actions on behalf of the 'liked' person by those who see him/her as similar.

Barack Obama, who became only the third African American Senator since the 1800s offered an explanation of his ability to connect with White rural and small-town voters. "I know those people," he said. "Those are my grandparents" (he spent his teen years living with his White grandparents in Kansas). "Their manners, their sensibilities, their sense of right and wrong – it's all totally familiar to me." Noam Scheiber argues that what makes Obama such a strong candidate outside the Black community is (an unthreatening) background – everything that serves to differentiate him from what White voters might see as stereotypically African American. ("The Candidate" *The New Yorker* May 31, 2004)

Secondly, "like-ness" facilitates *mentoring* and coaching relationships that guide individuals, provide critical and timely feedback, and give needed support as individuals navigate in organizations. Protégés are told which opportunities are best suited for them. They are given feedback that gives them insight into what is viewed as their strengths and weaknesses. Dr. Roosevelt Thomas says successful executives had mentors "who not only instructed them, but gave them career counseling and helped them make the right personal connections in the corporation."

One more point: Shared *networks* add the leader's name and credibility to the resume of the "liked person." When the promotion opportunity arises, all of these surrounding factors contribute to the final decision. They may not be the cause of the decision, but they are extremely influential.

The Example – Similarity+Mentoring+Networks = Promotions

In the early '90s I was working with Plaxon, a think tank for the U.S. government. Although there were only 2,100 employees, the organization's work was considered important to the Department of Energy and the rest of the government. Individuals who were successful at Plaxon usually went on to successful careers in the private sector.

I attended a going-away event for Robert, an executive who was also a great champion of the diversity and inclusion work at the agency. I stood in a room with 40-50 employees of Plaxon. There were nine African Americans and 14 White women. The rest were White men. Robert had hired the majority of the African Americans and White women, a fact he and the attendees were proud of.

At the event were three men in their seventies who were instrumental in Robert's success at Plaxon. Although these three men were about 15 years older than Robert, they could have been his relatives. All three were tall, slender, dressed in blue or gray suits, white shirts and subtle, patterned ties. The three of them took the stage together and, after a warm greeting, began to tell of Robert's journey in the company. Fred, who was Robert's first manager, described how they knew the minute Robert arrived that he would be successful. Fred reminded Robert that his advice about taking the job in engineering was the right counsel, even though Robert had resisted at first. Fred said to the audience, "If it had been up to Robert, he would still be a team leader in the quality control group."

Matt, who was Robert's "unofficial mentor" (Matt's words), told the gathering about how hard he was on Robert – insisting that he continually perform at higher levels. He shared that he did that because he *knew* Robert was capable of more and would move up the ladder.

The third gentleman, Brian, told the story of how he, without Robert knowing about it, gave him a project that would ultimately lead to Robert's promotion to director. Brian said he didn't want Robert to know how much was riding on his success with this project "because I worried he would turn it down."

"You see," he told us, "Robert never seemed to want to be as successful as we knew he could and should be."

Here were three powerful men who from the beginning of Robert's career at Plaxon pushed and pulled, smoothed and oiled his way to success. Did Robert have to prove himself, work very hard, and risk failure? Absolutely, but the chance to prove his worth was increased by the presence of these three men. They saw the potential (maybe because Robert reminded them of themselves or someone they knew) and made it possible for him to succeed.

"Cultural blindness represents the stage when the individual or organization actively proffers the notion that [characteristics] are inconsequential and of no importance." (Cross 1989) Cultural blindness would assert that Robert's race and gender and the similarity to the three benefactors was irrelevant to Robert's success, that none of the three "saw" that Robert was like them: White and male.

Facilitating Change

It is crucial that our leaders **Phillip** and **Victor** recognize that minimization and color-blindness interfere with an organization's ability to level the playing field and remove artificial barriers to equality and equity. In the corridors of the color-blind organization is a denial of privilege. The company remains unaware of practices that include or exclude. Moving individuals and groups beyond minimization will take time and focus.

Step One –   Make minimization and color-blindness a liability rather than a prize.

Step Two –   Raise the level of awareness about the nature and impact of privilege.

Step Three –   Identify the processes that facilitate equity – e.g., mentoring and coaching.

The organization and individuals in it are now ready to move to the fourth of the six stages, *Acceptance.*

Stage Four — Acceptance

This stage is marked by the knowledge that cultural diversity (differences and similarities) means different interpretations of similar behaviors. In the earlier example, at the stage of acceptance, Janet's hair has several possible meanings and will be interpreted differently based on diverse cultural notions. For Janet, her hairstyle is tied to convenience and culture (it is easy to find someone in the community to do the braiding). For her co-workers, her hairstyle represents a cultural statement (perhaps an indictment). For management, it represents an opportunity to address behaviors in a consistent manner, e.g., treating the braids the same way they treat an employee who dyes her hair blond.

Acceptance is a shift in perspective from "in my view" to "there are several possible views." In this scenario a curious colleague would be-

105

gin with the question, "Why do I care about Janet's new hairstyle?" He would view the answer to that question with honest curiosity about himself and his beliefs. The management's view would include the possibility that customers may care about Janet's hairstyle, but until there is evidence of an impact on clients, it is a non-issue.

Tools To Help Managers
Substitution

Substitution is the process of exchanging a situation or characteristic that I can comfortably and knowledgably work with for one I am less knowledgeable or comfortable with. For example, if a manager were trying to decide whether to discipline a minority employee for improper behavior, he could ask himself what he would do if the employee were a member of the majority. If I am trying to address a problem that deals with sexual orientation, perhaps I can substitute gender or age, subjects that I am more comfortable addressing to help guide my responses. In the case of Janet's hair, the manager using the tool of substitution would ask, "Did I call Mary into my office when she changed her hair color? If not, why would I call Janet in for changing the style?"

The STAE Model

This model illustrates a process that will increase acceptance by limiting assumptions and promoting education.

Stop
Think
Ask
Educate

Step One – **Stop assuming**. As William is about to judge Janet's hairstyle, he stops himself and acknowledges that any conclusions he has are based on unexamined assumptions.

Step Two – **Think.** What do I really know? Do I have any data to support my conclusions? What information do I have about the connection between culture, hairstyles and Janet's decision?

Step Three – **Ask questions**. I suggest that William ask potentially sensitive questions (if it feels awkward, it probably is) of friends or neighbors before asking colleagues. If there are no friends or neighbors to ask, that is data. The reason I suggest this approach is that it lets William explore the question of culture under less threatening circumstances and with less potentially negative workplace consequences.

Step Four – **Educate yourself**. If William uses the Internet (and who doesn't?) all he has to do is put "cornrow" in the search engine and he can gain interesting, useful and authentic information. Here's an enlightening result from just one Google® search on "cornrows":

Cornrows: Style & Substance

Almost any woman walking on 125th Street in Harlem will find herself in the midst of a strange courting ritual. It is not the catcalls, "hey-babys" and "can-I-walk-with-yous" that the corridor is famous for. It is instead this partly grating, partly soothing whisper of "hair braiding miss?" that echoes from West to East, up and down the north-south boulevards that cut across the meridian. The solicitors form clusters in front of bus stops and subway exits, ready to pounce on unsuspecting visitors. They are often impressive models of their own designs. It is sensible to begin any meditation on the cornrow here, in Harlem, and not because it is the so-called Mecca of the Black world or capital of African America, but because it is here that hair is so daily, publicly and insistently the center of a transaction. And this is fitting, for as much as cornrows are about Celebrating Our Cultural Heritage and Going Back to Our Roots, on the streets of Harlem as plied by cunning female immigrants from Senegal and Mali, all that cultcha is reduced to work. If for the customers "these styles represent a sense of harmony with both nature and the universe ... the African women's flawless sense of grooming" and can help "enhance and express your natural self" (as one hair braiding manual from 1973 put it), for every woman seen on the streets of Harlem asking: "Hair braiding miss? I give you good price ..." ad nauseum, the point isn't African survival in the anthropological sense, but African survival in the purest economic sense. Money made in the imagined Mecca of the African world gets sent back to that Africa of reality.

(By Sharifa Rhodes-Pitts)

Facilitating Change

- Provide information and opportunities for learning.
- Examine organization norms and practices to ensure that they are inclusive.
- Develop tools and techniques like substitution and the STAE model.
- Educate yourself and your colleagues. Continuously expand your cultural resources and knowledge base.
- Seek input from majority and minority sources and communities.
- Pay attention to and quickly respond to diversity-related issues.
- Get input from "cultural informants[xxxii]" e.g., focus groups, diversity councils and diversity teams. These groups can provide different perspectives.

An analogy I found interesting and relevant follows.

If we were traveling to a new destination about which we had little information, it is likely that many of us would consult travel agents, seasoned travelers, or residents of that particular locale. For the sake of discussion, if we were planning a trip to New York we might enlist the services of insiders to provide critical pieces of information that would facilitate our travel experience. For instance, we might inquire of the consultant whether we should arrive at Kennedy or LaGuardia airport, whether we should catch an airport shuttle, limousine, taxi or public transportation into the city. We would probably obtain recommendations about lodging. Should we stay in midtown or downtown Manhattan? Should we stay in an exclusive hotel or a moderately priced one? Insofar as restaurants, we might want to know whether we should dine at an ethnic restaurant, a deli or a restaurant that serves American cuisine. We might also inquire about entertainment. Should we visit a museum, the Statue of Liberty, Ellis Island or take in a Broadway play? All of these questions and many more would be addressed before we left the familiar surroundings of home. Consulting those who are more informed does not diminish our worth as individuals or lessen our potential as [leaders]. To the contrary, acknowledging areas in which we have limited amounts of information strengthens our competence [in those areas].[xxxiii]

In the journey toward cultural competency, it is advisable to seek information from individuals and groups who are familiar with cultures that might be new to us. This information is not gospel; it is advice based on familiarity. Additionally, at this stage human resource examines and revises policies that are culturally discriminatory. Diversity skills training and sexual harassment policy training are provided to managers and supervisors as companies hope to improve relationships. The organization modifies its recruiting strategy in order to increase diversity in the population.

Policies become more inclusive and less biased. Between 1990 and 2000 hundreds of companies changed their health care benefit policies. As they reached the stage of acceptance, many realized that their health benefit policies were unfairly discriminating against unmarried heterosexual domestic partners and gay and lesbian employees. The result was a significant increase in domestic partner and same-sex health care benefits.

Stages Five & Six — Adaptation and Integration

These stages can be described as cultural adaptation or bicultural competency. The individual and organization are capable of "walking in someone else's shoes" and understanding the fit. It is the generally accepted practice to value and encourage diversity at the individual and organizational levels.

Geert Hofstede's research defined cultural differences on five dimensions – power distance, uncertainty avoidance, individualism, masculinity and long-term orientation.

An individual who is adaptive not only recognizes her own cultural norms around individualism for example, but also is also able to assess her client country's cultural norms and subsequently acts appropriately in either culture. She understands that the U.S., her "home" culture, places a high value or rank on individual achievement and a larger number of loose interpersonal relationships. In her client culture, Singapore, individualism has a lower ranking, and collectivism and strong, close ties between individuals is more valued (Geert Hofstede™, 1967).

"Think of your frame of reference as an invisible window. Every-thing you see, touch, smell and hear must take place through your particular window. Some windows have a large frame that gives a broad view of what is going on outside them; others have a small frame that limits what can be observed."

(Cheryl Hamilton and Cordell Parker)

Facilitating Change

Identify where the organization and individuals are on the Competency Continuum.

| Stage 1 - Denial |
| Stage 2 - Defense |
| Stage 3 - Minimization |
| Stage 4- Acceptance |
| Stage 5 - Adaptation |
| Stage 6 - Integration |

Develop plans to move along the continuum. These plans need to include individual as well as organizational change.

If the organization is in Stage 1 – Denial or Stage 2 - Defense, immediate and considerable work is required. In Stage 3 – Minimization and Stage 4 - Acceptance, the work is more systemic and integrated. Once Stages 5 and 6 – Adaptation and Integration have been achieved, they must be continuously renewed – remember, it is a journey, not a destination.

Cultural Competency Continuum Journey

As the organization moves along the continuum attitudes, policies and practices reflect an appreciation for diversity and multiculturalism. Attitudes change to become less ethnocentric and biased. Policies change to become more flexible and culturally inclusive, and practices become more congruent with the organization's vision.

For individuals, the first step is to recognize that we have stereotypes, make unexamined assumptions and have mental models that lead to preconceived notions that are often flawed or incorrect. Multicultural competency lets us reject or avoid acting on preconceived thoughts, obtain new accurate information and resolve issues with confidence.

Head/Hands/Heart

Education has to develop knowledge, the head; behaviors, the hands; and attitudes, the heart. Knowledge without action or feeling may be interesting to the individual, but it holds no promise for change. Action that has no knowledge base and is without feelings is at best dangerous. And feelings without direction or mobility can lead to frustration and angst. It is the melding of the three that results in revolutionary change.

Developing multicultural competency is primarily knowledge based. Moving from *Minimization* to *Integration* requires the head and the hands: understanding and recognizing diversity, awareness of otherness and bicultural adaptation. Confronting one's cultural shortcomings and building multicultural strengths involves the hands: the behaviors and actions.

I believe a more important question is "What makes me *want* to learn or *want* to do something?" I think the *want* is the heart in the heads/hands/heart equation.

Developing the Heart

In the mid-'80s I was part of an HR team that organized a basketball game between DEC employees and members of a wheelchair basketball team (I'll call them the Rangers). The event was part of our Celebrating Differences program and was also a fund-raiser for the Rangers.

There were twelve members of the *real* basketball team and about twenty of us – engineers, personnel managers, systems analysts and designers. No one on my team had ever played basketball while sitting in a wheelchair. It is **much** harder than it looks. The first half the score was Rangers 46, DECees 4. (After halftime the Rangers switched scores with us and still beat us 58 to 50.) At halftime, the Ranger players joined their friends and family, and several of our team members got out of their wheelchairs and began to shoot baskets. I was livid! I yelled at two of my colleagues to "Get back in your chairs." They just looked at me as if I was nuts and continued to play. In my heart something felt wrong and out of place.

When the game ended, several of us from DEC went out for drinks with members of the Rangers and their spouses. We ruled out three of our local favorites because they could not accommodate seven wheelchairs. I asked if this was a common problem. They laughed at the absurdity of my question. I felt like Whites must feel when they ask Blacks if racial discrimination still exists. The answer is, "Of course!"

After a few drinks and stories about our kids, I asked two of the Rangers sitting next to me how they ended up "confined to a wheelchair" (I'll address learning about language a little later). Throughout the evening I was aware of feelings that ranged from curiosity to guilt, sadness to pity and always beneath it a profound discomfort. These young men (most of the team were 25-34) told us how they were doing normal, everyday chores like hanging Christmas lights or painting a ceiling when they slipped off the ladder and for the rest of their lives are *different*. One young man — he'd just turned 21 — was riding his motorcycle when a car struck it. Two others were injured in auto accidents. They talked of the difficulties of paying for the additional services required when a wheelchair is your mode of mobility. They described the depression that accompanies the reality when it finally sets in. They talked about uncomfortable reactions of friends and family members. And for those of us in HR, they addressed the lack of employment opportunities based on people's biases and prejudices, often masked behind accommodation challenges. I left the bar humbled and shaken. It was the first of many such experiences.

Training the Heart

Several years later I attended an incredible workshop designed and delivered by Don Zimmerman. I met Don while visiting a DEC plant in Phoenix Arizona. All of my colleagues were raving about this extraordinary trainer who was just like me and whom I would *love*. When I first met Don I wondered how my colleagues could see any similarities between us. Don was White and a quadriplegic who used a motorized wheelchair (the electric chair is used in Kentucky for really bad people). He was scrawny and balding. I will not lie; it took every ounce of diversity leadership to push myself through my initial discomfort, which fortunately lasted only thirty minutes. I discovered a funny, intelligent, extraordinary trainer who wanted to explore issues of race and disability for commonalities and differences. I also found one of the most outstanding workshop leaders I've ever had the honor to work with.

Don's two-day workshop entailed eight hours of classroom training designed to build participants' knowledge base. It was filled with information about language (people are not confined to a wheelchair – they get in and out of them), history (President Franklin Roosevelt was a paraplegic) and the legal side. We were required to read everything we could find on people with disabilities, companies' rights and obligations (this was two years before the Americans with Disabilities Act (ADA).

On day two we were told to meet at a large mall. When we arrived, each of us was given a wheelchair — our mobility for the next four hours. We were advised of the rules. 1) You could not tell anyone that it was part of a class and 2) You could watch only one movie (there were several theaters in the mall). What I learned in these four hours forever altered my heart. As an African American I'm used to being a racial minority. I was not prepared for how I was treated as a disabled minority. I watched people stare and point at us. I listened to people speak to me as if I had difficulty understanding English – they seemed to feel I had a hearing problem, so they spoke loudly and slowly. When I asked a question about a product or asked for help reaching something, people looked away and often blatantly ignored me.

The most significant event of the day required me to break the rules. While a colleague and I were having lunch at one of the fast food restaurants (another story for the next book) a woman asked if she could join us. We were surprised (it was so different from our earlier experiences) and gladly invited her to sit with us. When she sat down she said she needed our help.

Her Story

> *"About a year ago my daughter Deborah was injured in an accident and has been told by numerous medical doctors that she will never walk again. Deborah is extremely depressed and talks about suicide often. I've tried everything. She goes to*

counseling for a few weeks and then stops. Her therapist said I could have her committed to an institution if I believe she is a danger to herself, but most facilities aren't great for people in wheelchairs. When I saw your group, you all seem so happy and adjusted to being in wheelchairs, and I was wondering if you would be willing to come to my home and talk with my daughter. I think if she could see that other people who are like her are doing fine, maybe it would help her."

At the time of this story, my youngest daughter was twelve. I was deeply touched by the woman's words. I knew that what she must be going through as a mother who felt helpless to make her child feel safe, whole and happy had to be indescribably painful. We had to tell her our experience, unlike Deborah's, was temporary. When we said we were not disabled, and that this was a four-hour experience, she thanked us and quickly left the table. Don told us this was common, that people with disabled friends or family members often sought help from work-shop participants at the mall. The reason – here were disabled people who were happy and excited. Even though our hands were sore from pushing the chair, the knowledge that this was temporary showed on our faces. People wanted their loved ones to have the same look.

Isn't it enough to have the head and hands? No, the knowledge and skills are important but not sufficient to generate the magnitude of change needed to create a truly inclusive environment. In the early 1990s after the passage of the ADA I was at a drive-up (teller-less) ATM window at a branch of one of the largest banks in Massachusetts. I was reading the instructions and noticed that one set was in Braille. In order to complete the transaction you had to *visually follow instructions* on a screen. So why was the *drive-up* window set up with Braille in-structions and without audible cues? I believe it was because able-bodied individuals with "knowledge of the laws" based their actions on serving the law (the head) and providing "access" (the hands). Missing was the heart, the passion to make sure that blind and visually impaired banking customers felt included, welcomed and served.

The Rangers vs. DECees and the Disabilities Awareness workshops changed my heart, head and hands. The knowledge about disabilities alone was not sufficient to cause me to act, to insist that my clients in-clude disabilities in their definition of diversity and inclusion, and include physical abilities and limitations in the design of buildings and in practices and policies. There was more. Something had to touch my heart.

What type of work engages the heart, hands and head? It is the experience that is grounded in identifying, understanding and authentically addressing *privilege.*

Reading and following the ADA requirements will help an organization ensure that it is compliant with the laws. This is important. Understanding the Equal Opportunities Employment laws will put a company on the right road. Understanding the corporate policy on diversity and inclusion will lead an organization in the right direction. Knowledge of cultural competencies will help individuals and groups reach their initial targets.

Classroom education, articles, books and video training can close my knowledge gap. Assignments, on-the-job training and role-playing can develop my *hand* skills and cause new behaviors. I can put the instructions in Braille on the panel at the drive-up ATM.

What's missing is the heart. What's absent is my understanding of able-bodied privilege, the difference between my daily experiences and that of Robert, who uses a wheelchair. When I think only of my experience I am unaware of the "invisible package of unearned assets that I can count on cashing in each day."

An Educational Experience for Leaders' Heads, Hands and Heart.

While I was consulting to executives and the Executive Diversity Council at Airwelt, the CEO and I discussed the issue of employing the disabled. I had provided the leadership group with lots of education on the subject. He said he felt sure that Airwelt followed the letter *and* the spirit of the law. When the council came to its next meeting we had an educational experience that would teach their heads and hearts and ultimately influence their hands. All of the twenty-two leaders were given a "disability." The visually impaired had their eyeglasses covered with film. Eight had to use wheelchairs and were allowed to leave them only once inside the bathroom stall. Those with hearing impairments were fitted with soundproofing earplugs. Several wore slings, and two — the CEO and the council co-chair — had multiple disabilities. They were then asked to conduct the council meeting as planned. When asked how they could conduct the meeting "like this" I replied, "Disabilities often happen the night before a presentation (an eye injury or a fall that causes a broken leg), and when that happens companies don't cancel meetings."

About two hours into the workshop council members began to complain. "I can't see and it's giving me a headache," said one executive. "Can't I get a different disability?" My reply was, "If you suffered an eye injury, could you trade?" After six hours we returned to the privilege of being able-bodied and discussed our experiences. This was followed by a panel discuss and a question and answer session with six Airwelt employees with physical disabilities.

What Happened Next
The Head

Every member of the council talked about how the experience changed their perceptions about the significance of disabilities and the privilege of being able-bodied. When they were temporarily disabled, some became so frustrated they quit trying to be successful. Several of these individuals expressed surprise at how quickly being different could derail their efforts. Others talked about how easily they discounted those whose disabilities interfered with their goals. A woman of color manager who was temporarily hearing impaired said her small group finally stopped trying to include her in the conversation after her third request that they speak louder. When she pointed this out, her team members were taken aback by how quickly they could move from team focused to "me first."

The Hands

The council meeting was followed by a panel discussion with five Airwelt employees with disabilities. During the discussion, an employee told the group how difficult it was for her to take food from the cafeteria to eat at her desk on days when she was working on a time-sensitive project. She was an amputee and could not hold her tray and open the heavy cafeteria door. She described how she sometimes had to stand and wait for someone to come who could help her, and even though no one complained it was humiliating. Within a week after the session, the doors to the cafeteria were changed and a sensor automatically opened them when *anyone* approached. As the CEO put it, "For less than $500 we can ensure that no one has to wait and feel even slightly humiliated. That's a very small price to be an employer of choice."

The Heart

Today, six years later, the CEO brings up this experience as one that changed his life. Prior to this experience the concept of *privilege* was academic and intellectual. Everyone agreed that no one should have "an invisible advantage." All of the council members had read articles about disabilities and studied training material from an organization that specializes in disability awareness training. However, being disabled, even for a short time, affected them at the gut level. Even the knowledge that they would soon be able-bodied did not stop them from feeling frustration, discomfort, anger and self-pity. They understood on an emotional and intellectual level someone else's reality. From that point on "people with disabilities" was and would always be more than a phrase.

The fourth of the $^7K^2S$ is making sure there are numerous learning and educational opportunities along the way.

Education provides information that can shape what we know and how we behave. It can provide us with skills and will — experiences and information.

Education is key to the success of the diversity and inclusion journey because it fills the head with information, teaches the hands to act in a desired way and opens the heart to feel or believe in a desired way.

Education must:

Develop Multicultural Competencies – looking at the culture of the organization and understanding the impact that has on its people.

Provide Tools – ideas, activities and solutions that management can use in the middle of the daily insanity.

Provide Experiences – they're much more powerful than an article or a lecture to help me understand a concept.

These occasions come in many forms. A corporate executive can buy fifty tickets for her group to attend the African Dance performance and add attendance at this event to their metrics.

Your co-worker says she is observing Ramadan. You're searching the Internet for information (by the way, if you put *Ramadan* into Google® Search, it says there are 2,790,000 results), finding information at the library, contacting diversity Web sites that provide education, and talking with your co-worker about the religious observance. It's the willingness to make a *personal,* not just a professional or collegial, investment in learning.

If a team is working with colleagues in another country, they can agree to teach one another culturally relevant information.

When traveling to another country, colleagues can explore the notable and well-known places and the less known but interesting places. When I was in China I visited the Great Wall (the well-known learning experience) and I ran a 10K road race (the less known but intriguing experience). I did both in an effort to better understand the Chinese people and their culture. I grew up in Kentucky, and I know that my physical surroundings and my cultural mapping have shaped me. Here's what I learned from these distinctly different and unique experiences:

At the Great Wall:

- *Many Chinese people haven't visited the Great Wall (like many New Yorkers have not visited the Empire State Building, or Californians Disneyland). My Chinese colleague went for the first time when he took our group.*
- *The wall isn't what I think of as a wall – it's more like a stone bridge.*
- *You don't really climb to the top; it's 4,163 miles long. You walk for some distance and then turn around and walk back.*
- *A Black woman is an oddity. I am in the photos of thirty or forty people I will never see again. They put their arms around my neck and had their friends and family put me in their pictures.*

At the road race:

- *The forms are in Chinese, so I had to have someone translate them for me.*

- *They give you a T-shirt, which you must wear during the race.*

- *There is a starting order, and it goes by age and gender (the youngest go first) until you get to the Internationals. We start last no matter our age or gender.*

- *There is a time limit on finishing. If you leave your gear inside the stadium where you start, but you don't make it back in time, you're locked out until after the closing ceremonies. This isn't publicized, but another International told me. That's good to know since we started almost fifteen minutes after the first group and still had the same finish time limit.*

- *There are no water stops. That's 6.2 miles (10K) with no water. (It's possible there were water stops, but I didn't see them, and since my Chinese was limited to hello and goodbye I couldn't ask anyone.)*

- *The older Chinese men and women run faster than I do. At one point a woman who appeared to be 1,000 years old looked at me (as she passed me) and asked, "You OK?"*

- *The traffic isn't stopped, but the spectators are very encouraging.*

- *A Black woman runner is an oddity. People stare and point, but since I don't speak Chinese I just smiled and said hello.*

I visited the Great Wall because I was curious to see what it looked like. I learned much more than I imagined — about history, pride, families and an appreciation for tradition.

I signed up for the road race because I knew it could teach me something, but I didn't know what that was. I came away humbled, tired, thirsty and amused (at the treatment of the Internationals, as we were called).

Just being in a class on diversity doesn't make me knowledgeable. I can sit in a garage all day, but that won't make me a mechanic. It's what I do in the class and, much more important, what I do when I leave the course.

With a clear vision, articulate and committed leaders, visible support and an educated population, the organization is ready to measure individual's and the organization's progress.

Chapter seven

measurements

Measurements and Deliverables

When I travel on interstate roads in California I observe the speed limit because I've gotten three speeding tickets and each one came with an increasingly negative financial burden. When I'm driving through Nevada to Las Vegas I am free to drive as fast as I choose (I think they want me to get there quickly and give them all of my money) and I often choose to drive exceedingly fast. The danger of an accident and subsequent death (I drive a fast but small and fragile sports car) is about the same when driving exceedingly fast (95 mph) in Nevada and much slower (75 mph) in California. What's different is not my intelligent driving habits; it's the fact that what gets measured counts.

> *"What gets measured gets done."*
> *(Tom Peters)*

I think this notion is especially important to the diversity and inclusion journey. We live in the age of measurements and deliverables. "How fast can you download songs from the Internet?" "What was last year's return on investments (ROI)?" "What is the doctor to patient ratio in this hospital?" "What is our cost per hire?" Historically, diversity work has been categorized as *soft*, which is code for difficult to measure and track, and therefore easy to dismiss.

In 1997 Dr. Edward E. Hubbard wrote "Measuring Diversity Results," ten chapters, 210 pages dedicated to helping any organization learn what to measure and how to measure it. "If the language of businesses is dollars, then the alphabet is numbers. All organizations, whether profit or not-for-profit, depend on their ability to get the best possible return on dollars invested."[xxxiv]

Hubbard's book signaled the beginning of a brave new world where the financial reasons for creating an inclusive culture and having visible diversity joined the business' need for metrics and therefore deliverables.

Albert Einstein observed, "The significant problems we face cannot be solved at the same level of thinking we were at when we created them."

This is especially true where measurements and deliverables for the diversity and inclusion initiative are concerned. The challenge of measurements is twofold. On the individual level it is difficult to find the "baseline" from which progress is generally measured. At the organization level, measurements are difficult because of what we traditionally quantify and track. We have to find a new way of thinking about what we want.

The second dilemma is that once we create viable measurement tools, how do we correctly determine what the deliverables should be? Are there deliverables for individuals, management, leaders and teams? Do the deliverables change as the organization matures? And how do we establish deliverables that are meaningful to both the organization and to the individual?

Measurements and deliverables are the fifth of the Seven Keys To Success ($^7K^2S$). The organization has developed and communicated its vision. The leaders' behaviors indicate their support and commitment. There are groups and functions dedicated to supporting the initiative. There are multiple learning opportunities that provide employees and management with relevant information and experiences. Now it is time to hold people accountable for delivering on their promises and commitments. The organization is ready to establish what's expected at the individual and management level.

There are two challenges. The beginning — the baseline is essential for measurement — if I don't know where I started my journey, it's difficult to tell how far I've gone. And the end, it's difficult for me to establish my *goal*. Often, I don't know what I don't know. Both of these issues can be overcome, but only with conscious effort.

The Individual Dilemma

My first struggle is that I'm never sure how racially biased I was last year, so it makes it difficult to tell how far I've progressed. Whenever I ask people if they have racial, gender or religious biases, most respond with a resolute, "NO!" This denial changes as they become more aware of how to identify their prejudices and biases, but it makes it difficult to measure true change. On a scale of 1 to 1,000, am I a 63 or 630 today? If I can list only ten biases today, and as I learn more tomorrow I can list 35, does this mean I am getting better or worse? After all, I've gone from having a few to having more negative stereotypes or so it seems. I begin at the *unconscious incompetent* stage and progress to *conscious incompetence*. If you ask me to rate myself at the unconscious stage, I score much higher because I don't know what I don't know.

The process – To address this predicament I develop goals based on what I know about myself. These goals can be event based, educational or experiential. My early goal can be to attend three learning and educational events that will give me information about cultures or groups I know little about but are groups I will work with in the near future.

The deliverable – I am more culturally competent (for more on this see in chapter six) and less dependent on similarity. I increase my appreciation for and ability to work with diversity.

The Organization Quandary

At the organizational level our challenge is not that we don't know where we are; it's that what we measure seldom leads us to where we want to go. We measure what we can count, and that leads to a focus on race and gender in the U.S., plus gender, ethnicity and disabilities in other countries; therefore other dimensions of diversity get much less attention. We understand how to measure the number of disabled employees, women and minorities who are hired, terminated, promoted, transferred and any other activity that impacts these groups.

This leads us to hold managers accountable for their ability to positively impact numbers. We measure the number of ethnic minorities that managers hire. Some managers hire more than we expected and we reward them. Others hire the amount we set and we praise them for meeting their objectives. Still others hire fewer than we expected and we punish them for their failure. The deliverable becomes hiring them. Is that really the result we want?

All of our earlier work tells us this is not enough. By now, the organization understands that diversity is more than visible characteristics and that the important work involves diversity *and* inclusion.

If the only differences we measure (around the globe) are visible, while saying we understand the significance of the many invisible ones, we create conflict and even a distrust of the initiative.

> *"If you know why, you can figure out how."*
> *(W. Edwards Deming)*

So what should we measure? I suggest we measure what we want to change. We measure those things that lead us to the *why*. If you refer to your business case, many of things you want to change will point you in the right direction.

For example, if your business rationale is to avoid lawsuits, it's important to measure the variables that are most likely to help you do that. If you are a U.S.-based organization, ethnic minorities file the majority of lawsuits and the charges are discrimination in hiring and promotions. Applicable measurements include: progress in interview-to-hires, acceptances to offers, promotions for minorities and reduction in involuntary and performance-related terminations.

These measurements can provide you with ways to lower turnover, better educate and prepare interviewers and see interviewing, hiring or retention patterns early. You may, for instance, notice a pattern of higher turnover at a particular site, facility or in a specific management group. The earlier this is detected, the sooner the organization can develop deliverables and see positive results. Remember, what gets measured gets done.

If the business case is related to specific market segments, the measurements are focused on increased presence. You might build a baseline for the future market share in a particular market — the GLBT community, for example. The deliverables for the marketing and sales groups can focus energy on steadily increasing sales and market share in that community. This may be a time to engage or establish a GLBT network to help the sales force or provide ideas for marketing.

For those businesses whose goal is to be the workplace of choice, you might want to set a baseline at the current number of programs that increase employee satisfaction, e.g., work life initiatives, child care and dependent care help, and on-site services like dry cleaning and pharmacy. The deliverables may be increased utilization and can be measured by geography and group. Utilization is an important measure of the culture. Many organizations have job sharing and parental leave policies and practices, but the culture prohibits their use — either overtly or covertly. The goal could be to get greater use by rewarding managers and groups that use the services.

Often organizations want to change the makeup of the pool of candidates available for current and future openings. They want to see more diversity — ethnic, gender, racial, experience and/or background. In India it may be geography, or in the U.K. it may be nationality. If your organization wants to change the number of women in the interview pool (the underlying assumption is that more in the pool will result in more in the organization), we can measure individual and organizational behaviors and actions that will increase the likelihood that there will be more diversity in the pool. The metric can be as simple as increasing the number of informational interviews to increase the number of resumes available.

Organizations can use a "Best" list to monitor their progress and as a method of comparison. There are hundreds of lists such as:

Top 10 Companies for Recruitment & Retention.
Best Companies To Work For In India.
Best Companies for Minorities.
Best Companies for Women.
Best Companies for Gay and Lesbians.
100 Best Workplaces in the EU.

If we want to create more inclusive environments, it is important to measure elements that when present or increased will lead to more inclusive behaviors and actions. For example, we know that the first six months of employment are central to long-term satisfaction and success. The quicker employees are integrated into teams, the sooner they feel invested and valued, the sooner they can and will contribute. Having a mentor, coach or "buddy," someone to help one learn the written and — more important — unwritten rules, someone to share the early frustrations with and someone to help with the transition is crucial for future success. To increase the likelihood that this will happen, you can measure management and individual employees' efforts that impact this. For example, ask, "What is your level of participation in company-sponsored mentoring, buddy or coaching activities?" Or, "Are you a mentor, buddy, coach or sponsor for a new employee?" These questions from the 7Keys Scorecard® (See Appendix B for sample 7Keys Scorecard® questions) relate to inclusion and inclusive behaviors.

7Keys Scorecard®

One tool for measurements is the 7Keys Scorecard®. This scorecard differs from traditional measurement instruments in two fundamental ways. First, many scorecards are designed for managers only. With the 7Keys Scorecard® there are three different scorecards for organizations to use. They can be used to establish measurables and deliverables for all employees — senior managers of groups and functions, managers of individual contributors and small teams and individual contributors.

The individual contributor scorecard measures the amount of energy employees expend doing things that increase their multicultural competency and comfort with diversity. It measures actions that support the organization's diversity and inclusion journey. It measures how often they take advantage of learning opportunities offered internally and externally. Additionally, the employee scorecard gives individual contributors on the shop floor and in the offices a measurement tool that can be incorporated into the performance review process.

The second way that the 7Keys Scorecard® differs is it does not emphasize metrics based on the classic notions — hires, promotions and terminations of women and minorities. There are numerous tools available to measure progress on these dimensions.

As an alternative the two manager scorecards measure personal as well as leadership behaviors. It does not measure the number of hires; it measures the actions that lead to high quality hiring, promotions, development and retention of diverse talent – things like informational interviews, attending events that promote networking with *new and different* talent and activities like mentoring and coaching. Additionally, the 7Keys Scorecard® measures managers' knowledge of what *their* managers are doing, which allows them to establish metrics and deliverables for the performance review cycle.

The 7Keys Scorecard® also increases the visibility of the diversity and inclusion journey. It lets leaders track how often the diversity initiative is shared throughout the organization. The scorecard tracks how often the journey is mentioned in meetings. It assesses whether mangers are making diversity and inclusion a regular part of their agenda and not a *special* meeting topic (remember, budgets, customers, clients, service, quality and profit aren't special; they are a part of who we are). It measures the level of support that employees are giving to the journey and to one another. This is essential because the initiative has to be visible to be successful.

The scorecard measures diversity in the largest context – more than race, gender and other visible characteristics. This reinforces the notion of the inclusivity of the initiative. Individual contributors and managers are offered ways to join the journey that fit their lifestyles and work styles. People can explore cultural diversity to satisfy future work demands, curiosity or an external need (often someone is in school or enrolled in a degree program and can use this learning to satisfy an academic need).

"Improvement is not achieved by focusing on results, but by focusing on improving the systems that create results."
–(National Leadership Network)

Using Metrics

A StarrCom executive was searching for "something tangible" for his organization. The 7Keys Scorecard® fit the bill. It offered his organization actions, and metrics that were easy to understand and track. He began the process by discussing with his leadership team the desired outcomes, the why and the process. He completed his scorecard and developed his plan with goals and a timetable with his CEO. The rollout began with his team members completing their scorecards, discussing their strengths and weaknesses with him and developing their measurements and goals for the next twelve months. Each leader clearly understood what she/he was expected to do as an individual and as a manager. Over the next twelve months this organization rolled out the 7Keys Scorecard® and ninety-seven percent of the employees enrolled in this process.

The 7Keys Scorecard® was integrated into the performance review process of the 700+ employees. The results were amazing. Recruiting costs were reduced by almost 25%. Retaining talent became easier. The employee feedback in meetings, focus groups and surveys indicated that many of the activities generated by the scorecard positively impacted employee satisfaction, management skills and teamwork.

Now it was not the cure for cancer, but it had a significant impact on everything from the organization's growth in understanding and capturing emerging markets to individuals' comfort with diversity and inclusion issues.

You can measure those things that lead to desired outcomes and you can measure outcomes. Once you have clearly articulated the business case, define the things you measure based on what you view as important contributors. For instance, if expanding your business into new markets is one of the *main things*[xxxv] the hiring of employees with knowledge of the expanding markets can be measured as an outcome – you can count the number of new employees with knowledge of the expanding markets. You can also measure the behaviors that lead to identifying new markets such as membership in organizations with a concentration of members with an understanding of the new markets.

What gets measured gets done *and* what gets done should be rewarded.

Every year StarrCom managers select five to eight employees whose work has supported the diversity and inclusion journey, and each receives $7,500 in December. The employees and their manager or supervisor are brought together, and the CEO presents the checks. Their pictures and their contributions are then featured in the in-house publication.

Rewards are important. The measurement system and rewards for achieving the goals must be visible, inclusive and integrated. However, if what you want is creativity and not processes, be careful what you measure and what you reward.

"When people feel that they are being rewarded for an activity, that feeling of external control is enough to actually impair creativity. Explicit rewards, then, can be an effective way to kill off our creativity. If (internal drive) is high, if we are passionate about what we are doing, creativity will flow."

(Frans Johannson)

You don't need to use the 7Keys Scorecard®. Whatever tool you choose, it is important to remember that success is achieved through performance. It is not enough to measure activities. You must measure results, those that move the organization toward its goals. Measure those things that when performed well will increase the success, health and longevity of the organization.

Chapter eight

everyone's in

A Modern Day Fable for Business ©

Once upon a time, an up-and-coming corporation explored the world looking for the best and brightest people. Although the firm worked hard developing equipment and procedures, it had never taken the time to prepare its workers or managers for the reality of business in the second millennium. And so, this business, which should have been leading the way, became a sleek, well-tuned rowboat adrift in a sea of competition. It had a crew and someplace to go, but it just didn't have the skills to get it there.

One day, the "different" employees were fed up. Some of the disgruntled rowers, who were tired of being labeled affirmative action hires, decided to jump up and down in the front of the boat. This caused the boat to rock back and forth, making some of the rowers in the back feel nauseous and off-balance. Others, who were sick of being passed over for promotions and always having to be the ones to make the coffee (but who have been taught as small children never to make waves), smiled and rowed backward, causing the boat to turn in circles.

Rowers who felt ostracized because of whom they loved or lived with, started secretly drilling little holes in the bottom of the boat. Those who were diligently rowing began to notice that their shoes and socks were getting soaked. They had to row and bail, slowing them down and making it difficult to concentrate. And the "challenged" workers, who had not been given any adapted tools, were being paid to row, but without accommodations they could only sit and watch.

Older rowers who were told they were "slow and stuck in their ways" loaded their pockets with heavy rocks and smiled at each other because now they really were slower. The extra weight caused the boat to sink deeper and move at a snail's pace.

Another group, the majority rowers, selected from the best schools, trained to row tirelessly, discovered that not only were their behinds getting wet, but also they were the only ones rowing — so they quit. And now that corporation, with all of its slick technology, processes and magnificent equipment, that was primed to go someplace fast was spinning and rocking out of control.

And then the owners, managers and rowers all looked at each other and wondered why with so much potential, knowledge, skill and energy they were being outpaced by their competitors, drained of their talent and going nowhere, except maybe under.

The End

Understanding Participation

Everybody has to participate if the initiative is to have any chance to succeed. When people drop out because they don't feel included or valued, those who are left are burdened with additional duties and responsibilities. Eventually, everyone participates or everyone quits!

So why do some people willing get on board, put themselves in situations that they know beforehand will make them uncomfortable and commit their time and energy to the diversity and inclusion journey? Why do most efforts begin with a nucleus of less than one percent of the population and often only eight to ten people? What makes one CEO embrace inclusivity and see it as an imperative while thousands of others seem to wait in the wings for direction or orders? Why do some people continue to row when their shoes and behinds are wet while others quit before they even touch the oars? Because they notice that there is a seat with their name on it. The initiative is designed with them in mind.

Remember Emma Goldman? "If I can't dance it's not my revolution."

I believe the truest measure of the success of an organization's diversity and inclusion journey is how many people have joined along the way – how many people can dance. The initiative that captures the hearts and minds, the passion of most if not all employees will be the most successful. Why?

Participation is an indicator of understanding.
Participation is a measure of the visibility, inclusivity and integration of the initiative.
Participation is contagious.

Participation is an indicator of understanding.

People support ideas, causes and initiatives with a personal benefit that they can relate to. The more I understand about the initiative, the more likely I will embrace it. Early in the journey, diversity and inclusion can appear to be complex and mysterious. As knowledge, understanding and appreciation for diversity and inclusion grow, so does the participation of more and more employees.

In the early stages everyone asks, "Why are *you* doing this to *us*?" This question is an indication that the business imperative is unclear. When employees see that the changing face of business means new faces sitting next to them – in India or Indiana, new faces using their products and services and new faces bringing fresh ideas, the "why are you doing this to us" becomes "what should *we* be doing?"

The more **we** understand that the *value of diversity* is the fact that truly innovative and creative solutions to the challenges our organizations face come from the diversity of our cultures, experiences and interactions, the easier it is to get everyone to row together.

Understanding can be measured by employees' participation in support or learning efforts (e.g., joining networks, affinity groups, and book clubs, or attending educational events), for the more I understand about the power of diversity and inclusivity, the more I want to make it a reality on my team and in my group.

Participation indicates visibility.

When the leadership talks about the journey – its importance to the organization's future and the leaders' support for it — participation increases. A major reason for the success of the Safety First Initiative at

Niontek was the level of visibility. Participation stemmed from the fact that the initiative was visible everywhere you looked and in every message you heard.

In order for employees to understand and appreciate the value of diversity and inclusion, management must be able to answer **yes** to these questions:

- Do my/our direct reports know which way we are headed and what needs to happen next?
- Is this journey a part of every message I/we deliver?
- Do our clients, customers, vendors and suppliers know how important this is to us and are they clear about their responsibilities to help us achieve it?
- When I/we visit any of our buildings, is there a clear indication of the importance of this journey?

Participation is a measure of inclusivity

Inclusion refers to practices that actively and passively persuade individuals and groups that they are a part of the whole and expected to contribute, to have a say and to help direct the efforts of a team, group or organization.

If all of the effort is focused on leaders and managers, it is not likely that non-managers will participate. If the resources, activities and efforts of the initiative are concentrated within fifty miles of corporate headquarters, there will be little involvement from people outside that fifty-mile radius. If the initiative appears to support one group to the exclusion of another, members of the "other" are less likely to contribute as much as they could.

If the journey is not inclusive, the single-no-children employee who feels like he is strapped with an increasing and never-ending workload because, as he tells us, "Three of my colleagues have taken maternity leave in the past year and two others are pregnant. And because I don't have children they think I don't deserve any time off" will not row. When the initiative includes *work and life balance* and not just *work and family balance* we will search for ways to make the environment more worker friendly rather than simply family friendly.

How do you make sure your initiative is inclusive?

Reflect diversity and inclusivity issues in all policies and practices.

Seek input and participation from all areas of the organization and from all segments of the population.

Participation indicates integration.

Make sure the *ends of the threads are invisible*. When the goal for organizations is to have the diversity and inclusion work at its finest, it is impossible to tell where the initiative begins and ends.

Demonstrate that *diversity* is in everything we do; it is more than a day or a luncheon.

Show how it is in our products, marketing, client and customer service and the way we do business.

It is in our presentations, our buildings, hallways and plant sites.

Inclusivity is who we are as well as how we operate.

Participation is contagious.

The secretary who is a member of the Hispanic Employee Network infects her colleagues with her enthusiasm. She talks about what the group is doing. She shares what she learns about how important it is for the company to build its brand and include the emerging market of Latino and Hispanic consumers. She tells stories about growing up different and what that meant to her. She brings in books for others to share with their families. She is so enthusiastic about the Puerto Rican Day parade that several of her co-workers and their families join her. They get permission, and eighty-five employees wearing T-shirts with the organization's logo represent the company.

Managers who initially resist the initiative because they do not feel it will include them become the loudest and most vocal supporters when they discover the satisfaction they derive from mentoring talented minorities. As one executive said, "I get more out of the relationship than I give. I've told several of my colleagues that they don't know what they're missing. I started with just one protégé, and now I have four."

Pros of participation.

Remember the train? The initiative must provide a place for everyone to get on board and travel with the company, not leaving some people behind or alienating others. The company where everyone is rowing and contributing will have more brainpower working for, rowing with it, rather than against it.

The Giant

Several years ago I visited a large video chain. I was looking for a particular movie on DVD. The video store had thousands of titles on VHS, but only a few on DVD. When I asked a clerk why they had so few DVD movies he said, "I just work here." My curiosity was tweaked and I began to study the video store market. I discovered that in Southern California, there were hundreds of mom and pop video rental places. There were those that rented Spanish title videos and those that had movies in Vietnamese. There were stores that catered to the gay and lesbian market. There was a new service that let the Internet-savvy consumer rent DVDs with fewer complications and greater choices. Individually, none of these services or stores could rival the large chain, but collectively they were eating away at the giant's markets and profit.

What happened? On paper the large chain has a diverse workforce. The company has gay and lesbian salespeople, talented Hispanic and Latino store managers and technically competent professionals. Why then was the firm unable to get in front of the changes? Maybe it did not accommodate its talent. Perhaps the gay and lesbian employees couldn't find a comfortable seat on the train where they could think about ways to help their company bring in their friends. Perhaps there were no poles for their techies to play on while they discussed the reality of changes in technology. If everyone had had a comfortable way to connect, perhaps these employees might have helped the company see that the future was multilingual, DVD-based and on the Internet. Today, that large chain is trying to recapture the markets it has lost and at great financial cost.

When everyone participates in the journey, more people contribute to the business bottom line. The LaMaxxe Inc. example (from chapter three) shows what's possible when employees, in this case the gay and lesbian employee network, focus on helping the company attract new business.

Cons of Participation.

It will *feel* out of control. It may seem like there is no plan. In order for almost everyone to participate in the journey, there will be lots of activity, energy, effort and action. There will be weekly events. There may be networks for between ten and thirty groups — Christians, GLBT, women, Blacks, Hispanics, Asians, White men, disabled employees, Muslims and working parents, to name a few. You can expect to have an Executive Diversity and Inclusion Council, Regional Councils, Local Councils and Functional Councils. Activities like book clubs, film series, speakers, entertainment, cultural celebrations, multicultural luncheons and experiences (e.g., visits to museums) are common.

Some individuals will participate in a few and others in almost all of the sponsored events. Teammates may complain that people are not doing their share of the *real* work or are being given special treatment because they are _____ (fill in the blank). Managers may feel like their hands are tied – how can they tell a disabled employee she can't attend an event sponsored by the Disabled Employee Network without seeming like he/she doesn't support the diversity effort?

This is predictable. As the initiative matures, the efforts will become more integrated and congruent.

Caution: Do not let this temporary time of chaos derail your effort and commitment. Have faith in the process – the correctness of the journey and the greatness of one another.

faith

Faith

In the final analysis, there is a leap of faith that everyone in the organization must make. Somewhere around Year Three of the seven-to-ten-year journey it becomes necessary to believe that the light at the end of the tunnel is not a subway car about to run over you.

It's easier to make the leap of faith when you can read the map, when you have credible information that lets you know what to expect. This is not blind faith; it is faith based on drawings and diagrams created by hundreds of pioneers who have traveled the roads you are on.

The Three Stages

In every journey are three stages of development:

Awareness

The first two years of the journey. Characterized by turmoil, resistance and concerns. It requires patience and perseverance.

The most important elements are the first two keys – the business case and the behaviors of leaders.

Application

Years Two to Five of the journey. Characterized by understanding the value of diversity.

This stage is filled with activity.

137

Incorporation

Years Six to Ten of the journey. Characterized by integration into all of the processes and practices.

This becomes the time of the invisible thread. Diversity and inclusion are woven into the fabric of the organization.

Stage One – Awareness

This stage occurs during Year Zero to Two of the journey.

The first year of the journey is almost always a nightmare! Yes, prepare for the first year to be similar to having a puppy. It looked so cute in the window. You wanted it, bought it, paid for it and have great hopes for the days when you and your dog can sit by the fireplace and have the Hallmark® moment. But between that day and the reality of life with a three-month-old puppy are many moments of torment. In Year One, there is chaos, anger, resentment, elation, concern, relief and resignation.

There is competition between groups to hold onto power and acquire emerging power. This is the phase when those who have been in the powerful majority often become concerned and even afraid that the initiative will result in loss – of status, perks and privilege. Minority groups will often engage in turf fights as individuals come to grips with their own and others' similarities and differences.

It is essential that the organization's reason for traveling on this journey is clear to all and that the reason is inclusive and not exclusive. This is the time to establish short and long-term goals, measurements and expectations.

Whether there are 50 employees or 50,000, the topic is new, and curiosity, expectations and resistance are high. During Stage One, the most important factors are the first two Keys – connecting the success of the initiative to the achievement of business goals and the significance of the leadership's behaviors. If there is no Hallmark® moment on the horizon, no clearly articulated benefits, the time, resources and investments required will feel daunting and wasteful.

Additionally, if the leaders' behaviors do not clearly indicate their commitment to the long-term change process, the journey will become tedious, unfocused and ultimately fail. That may seem like a strong statement, but everyone has stories of organizations that embarked on this journey without the leadership walking the talk. I have heard of only one instance when the initiative was successful without the leadership, and hundreds where it failed. I'm not sure I'd want to bet my company's hard-earned resources on being the exception to the rule.

"You have to 'walk the talk.' The CEO and other executives must actively and conspicuously champion diversity in order to make it a priority within the rest of the company."
(Michael Landel, Sodexho)

If you have clearly communicated the direction and the expected behaviors, by the middle of Year Two, things have settled down. The puppy has stopped chewing through every pair of your shoes and socks, is house-trained and can walk on a leash. The organization has gone through the initial shock and excitement stage. There is a shared understanding of the business case – of why the organization is spending time, money and energy on becoming more diverse and inclusive. This is accomplished through communication, education and measurements. Often, early-stage affinity groups have formed (formally or informally), and there is an Executive or Corporate Diversity and Inclusion Council. Human resources has begun to develop more inclusive processes, e.g., expanded college recruiting to increase minority representation in the interview pool and flex-time policies for working mothers (usually at this point it's about mothers and not parents).

There has been some training (generally known as awareness training) for managers and supervisors. This training focuses on defining diversity and inclusion, understanding biases or mental models and filters, and some focus on behaviors that will be needed as the workplace becomes more diverse. The training course may be classroom or Web-based and will range from two hours to two days. As I noted in the chapter on Education, the training focus is on getting the biggest return for the money. The message is "get as many people as possible *through* the diversity training in the shortest time possible," rather like a mandatory inoculation or, as I sometimes think of it, "flea dipping": a process designed to help fix an immediate problem, but without proper care and follow-up, the "fleas" reappear in a few days.

Year One to Two — An investment in a well-developed and high-quality educational map will pay extra dividends. The earlier managers understand the depth and complexities of leading and engaging a diverse workforce, the smoother the journey. A map with markers, signposts, rest stops and checkpoints will provide direction that doesn't start at the door of the building, go one block and stop. Without this roadmap managers find themselves in the desert of diversity, alone, lost and angry. They feel betrayed by the organization and unable to avoid looking bad.

The Awareness Stage introduces the breath of diversity to the organization. Initially the focus may be on visible diversity – ethnicity, gender and age — but quickly it becomes apparent that diversity involves much more. It not only is about more characteristics than originally thought, including thinking style, personality, first language, sexual orientation, communication patterns and physical abilities, but it is also about the interaction between these characteristics. Managers who prefer brief, succinct communication will find themselves frustrated with the long-winded employee whose style is to examine each detail. Employees may dislike the smell of food that a teammate likes to warm in the microwave, or find the body odor of another employee offensive. They will bring these concerns to the manager with the same level of seriousness once reserved for conversations about racism. At this stage the depth and breath of the issues in a changing workplace can feel overwhelming, hence the "nightmare."

The good news about this stage is that many employees will embrace the organization's effort to create a more inclusive workplace. Acknowledging diversity lets individuals feel more open to express themselves. It helps teams begin to see that there may be resources in their group that they were unaware of or did not fully utilize. It is common for teams to discover that a member has a valuable skill or expertise that was previously hidden (intentionally or unintentionally).

I was consulting to an organization where several team members were having problems with their German colleagues' accents when working with technical specifications. During a discussion of backgrounds they discovered that an African-American on their team was fluent in German. He volunteered to help with the interpretation and to teach his team members some German words – this is the value of diversity.

Individuals begin to discuss their backgrounds and discover commonalities that improve working relationships. Parents - gay, straight, single and foster, bond around the challenges of raising children and contributing 110% to the organization. They may develop innovative ways to help each other balance the load without impacting their productivity or increasing costs.

OK, so you made it through the "puppy" years – the first two years of the journey.

Stage Two — Application

Stage Two occurs between Years Two and Five.

The organization has embraced the notion of diversity. There is awareness that individuals and groups have unique talents and an understanding that taking advantage of these distinctive capabilities can be beneficial and challenging. It is clear to the employees that diversity and inclusion are important to the future of the group. The resistance that was experienced in Year One has significantly diminished and been replaced by curiosity, engagement and interest. That is not to say that everything is rosy. As with all evolutionary processes, there are times when progress is replaced by stasis or regression, but that's temporary now. Although the puppy may sometimes resist walking on the leash, it takes only a few minutes before it settles down and learns new skills.

Years Two to Four — This is the most chaotic time. Unlike the first stage that is replete with resistance, in Stage Two it seems like everyday everyone is engaged in some part of the diversity effort, from training to workshops to networks to discussion. The organization's resources may become (in the opinion of some) overtaxed. Affinity groups form, storm, norm and begin to perform. Teams spend more time listening to the ideas of all members – some of whom have styles that make decision-making more difficult or time consuming. There are conferences, seminars, recruiting fairs and interviews that take time previously devoted to product or process issues. Internal and external groups ask for or demand financial resources as well as time and attention. Participation in charity events, parades, dinners, breakfasts, celebrations and the like can tax even the most ardent supporters of the initiative. Executives are asked to speak at fundraisers. Managers are expected to attend events, participate on panels, lead discussions at their staff meetings *and* produce at higher levels with fewer resources.

There are also numerous payoffs during this time. This is the time when the differences and similarities are applied to making the business more successful than it would be without them. The racial and ethnic diversity in the organization becomes the catalyst for and support of emerging markets. Networks or affiliation groups help with recruiting and retention. Focus groups provide information that helps managers and supervisors better understand the challenges and opportunities for "like" group members. The way LaMaxxe Inc. used its gay and lesbian employee network to increase its presence in the GLBT market is an example of how diversity is applied to the business. The application will vary by group and organization, but there are numerous ways the organization can benefit from its diversity, ways it can apply diverse ideas, markets, solutions and talents to help it solve complex problems.

Years Four to Five — This is the time of justifiable joy. On the individual level employees have a foundation for diversity and inclusion that lets them enjoy their own and others' diversity.

Six years after coming to work at StarrCom, a young Muslim woman felt comfortable enough to wear her head covering to work. She was featured in an article in the company newsletter where she talked about how the organization's diversity journey made her feel like it was safe for her to be herself and be identified with her religion. She also acted as a consultant to help the company produce an educational program focused on better understanding the Islamic religion. Her efforts significantly improved cross-cultural relationships and communication.

At Niontek a transgendered man had a conversation with his team about his upcoming visible transition from male to female and provided education so the team members would better understand what he was going through and why. When I asked him why he talked with them about this, he said he wanted to minimize the disruption on the team and give people time to get comfortable with his appearance changes. He said, "I don't expect everyone or even most of them to embrace what I'm doing, but I think it'll be easier if it's in the open and they have some resources to understand it."

On the management front Years Four to Five are easy. It is easier to recruit new talent because there are more avenues and helpers. Retention is easier because focus groups, affiliation groups and networks provide insight and direction into the things that make employees stay and those that make them leave. Issues like work and life balance have surfaced, and the organization has helpers in place. Teams have gone through the rough times and are better able to address issues of diverse style and ways of operating.

There is an understanding that global business is more than just buildings in other countries; it is a unique knowledge base that is a valuable resource. There is awareness that ideas can come from everywhere and there is richness to the texture of diverse organizations.

There are fewer lawsuits. There is less negative press, less turnover, shorter time to market and fewer global issues.

There are more positive interactions between people, recognition for their efforts and a better understanding of the emerging markets.

"In every word that I speak, every decision that I make, every communication and action I take, I must show the world that I am committed to diversity."

(Dr. Vance Coffman, Lockheed Martin Corp.)

Stage Three – Incorporation

This stage goes from Years Six to Ten.

It involves imbedding diversity and inclusion into the fabric of the organization. At this stage diversity is not a segmented topic or a separate initiative; it is a part of the daily life of the organization. Diverse opinions are sought. Diversity of ideas is the norm.

Individuals are culturally competent. They are courageously introspective. They understand how biases influence behaviors and inclusion.

Managers incorporate diversity into all of their practices — team building, recruiting and retention, measurements and rewards, promotions, education and training and benefits.

The organization views its diversity as one of the assets that distinguish it from its competitors and helps it continue to be successful. Leaders' behaviors reflect their commitment to inclusion, one of the strongest threads in the fabric of the organization.

"If I were to define a legacy, it would be that diversity is truly embedded in the fabric of the company. It's part of our thought process; we do it naturally, because it is part of what we are."

(Phillip Condit, Boeing Company)

Chapter ten

in conclusion

One rainy night a reporter interviewing A.J. Muste, who during the Vietnam War stood in front of the White House night after night with a candle, asked, "Mr. Muste, do you really think you are going to change the policies of this country by standing out here alone at night with a candle?" Muste replied, "Oh, I don't do it to change the country, I do it so the country won't change me."

(Andrea Ayvazian)

I wrote this book not so much to change the world, but so that the world with all of its resistance, procrastination, prejudice and cynicism does not change me. My love for this work grows each time someone "gets it." My passion is fueled by the diversity leader who reports that everything she does is influenced by her leadership in this discipline and the two leaders who work together to solve their management challenges – one Black, one White, both leaders *first.*

"Do business organizations really need to attend to diversity issues? Only if they intend to stay in business. Any company that believes it can ignore diversity concerns and still thrive in the modern global environment – which is diverse by definition – is set on a disastrous course."xxxvi

It is not **easy**, but it is **possible** to create and maintain a visibly diverse and inclusive environment that is filled with magical ideas, dedicated rowers and culturally competent leaders.

Personnel determine the potential of the team.
Vision determines the direction of the team.
Work ethic determines the preparation of the team.
Leadership determines the success of the team.

(John C. Maxwell)

Seven Keys to Unlocking the Passion for Diversity

- **The vision comes first**. A clearly articulated business case that engages and motivates all employees is vital. The vision should be alive and future focused. This is the foundation of the diversity and inclusion journey. It must be clear, easy to remember, simple to communicate, repeated until anyone can recite it and fit it on a T-shirt.

- **The visible and consistent leadership commitment follows.** Leaders must make footprints that others can follow – not small and shallow, but large and deep so that they can be seen from the top floor of the building. The leader who demonstrates the passionate commitment to diversity and inclusion will generate passion in all who have been looking for someone to follow. At this point the initiative will begin to generate its own momentum.

- **Everyone needs help.** It takes seven to ten years and the intelligent help of many to get it right. It is essential to have knowledge, energy and ideas — strategic and operational guidance on the journey. Participation engages hands, hearts and minds, spreads the strengths and provides the leadership with valuable resources.

- **Learning, education and training prepare us.** They come in many forms: passive, active, technological and interpersonal. They can take place in the classroom, the local museum, on conference calls and on Web site visits. Learning, education and training can be exciting and interesting. The local Gay Pride Parade, the photo exhibit and the Chanukah celebration can move us from unconsciously incompetent to culturally competent. They offer opportunities that energize employees' curiosity.

- **What gets measured gets done.** Measure your progress based on what you want to achieve. Don't measure what others measure unless you have the same needs they do. Measurements will evolve with the initiative.

- **Everyone rows.** Everyone participates. There's room and a seat at the table for everyone. Get people involved. Give them hundreds of ways to join the journey. Make it fun. Ignite their passion and their intellect.

At some point we know that it will work. We just have to close our eyes and make a leap of faith – like kids jumping into a pile of leaves in the fall.

Anyway[xxxvii]

People are often unreasonable, illogical and self-centered;
Forgive them anyway.
If you are kind, people may accuse you of selfish, ulterior motives;
Be kind anyway.
If you are successful, you will win some false friends and some true enemies;
Succeed anyway.
If you are honest and frank, people may cheat you;
Be honest and frank anyway.
What you spend years building, someone could destroy overnight;
Build anyway.
If you find serenity and happiness, they may be jealous;
Be happy anyway.
The good you do today, people will often forget tomorrow;
Do good anyway.
Give the world the best you have, and it may never be enough;
Give the world the best you've got anyway.

You see in the final analysis, *it is between you and God;* it was never between you and them anyway.

Appendix A

Answers to the questions

"I've done everything I can to motivate my managers to meet their diversity goals. Some of them seem to get it, but most of them don't. I really don't think it's because they don't want to; I just think they have a lot to do and it's hard to focus on this."

a. Articulate the vital connection between the success of the organization and the diversity and inclusion journey. Discuss the business case motivation – fear/avoidance, fairness/justice, marketplace opportunities, workplace of choice or a combination.
b. Model the behaviors you expect from others. When you demonstrate what you are doing to achieve your goals, it is easier for those who work for you to do the same.
c. Hold managers as accountable for achievement of diversity and inclusion goals as with other business goals, i.e., customer satisfaction, time to market and budgets.

"Where do you learn how to pay attention to diversity without stereotyping? I'd like to find out what the issues in my group are, but I don't want the liability attached to it. I'm at a loss and have no idea where to go or even what I need."

a. Use existing company or group resources. If there are employee networks or affinity groups, meet with them to discuss issues that have been raised and receive ideas about how to address them.
b. Host employee focus group sessions. Invite groups of ten employees to an informal breakfast or lunch to discuss three questions:

   1) What is working well as relates to diversity and inclusivity?
   2) What could use some improvement as relates to diversity and inclusivity?

> 3) What can you contribute to our diversity and inclusivity efforts?

    c. Attend an awareness training session to learn ways to avoid stereotyping.

    d. Practice the STAE Model and Substitution. (See Tools For Managers in chapter six.)

"Who do I go to with a diversity problem? HR doesn't have the answers, and legal says there's nothing they can do to help since it's not a policy issue. My senior manager doesn't know any more than I do."

    a. Clarify the "diversity problem." Often what has been identified as a diversity problem is a management problem, e.g., poor communication between individuals, inconsistent treatment that looks like discrimination or lack of clear expectations and goals. Identify the root issue.

    b. Seek more knowledgeable colleagues and superiors. Ask for help from other managers who have demonstrated cultural competency (see Multicultural Competency in chapter six).

    c. Discuss the "problem" with identified diversity and inclusion leaders – Caution: Follow employee confidentiality and privacy policies.

"I'm at the end of my rope over performance issues with three of my five minority employees. I think the reason they are failing faster than others (non-minorities) is we've lowered our interview standards but the customer still expects the highest level of service. I think we have to go back to hiring people based on talent and skill and not diversity."

    a. Ask yourself this question: "If I can hire talented White people and talented men, why can't I hire talented women or people of color?" The answer cannot simply be that women and people of color are not as smart as majority men. The more you understand about hiring talented majority employees (other than I just hire my relatives) the easier it will be to hire talented *people.*

    b. Look for root causes such as a limited Rolodex of potential minority talent and environmental issues like family and work balance issues that may have greater adverse consequences for minority group members.

c. Work with HR and recruiting to ensure that the interviewing standards are consistently adhered to, but be careful – often we raise the bar based on our biases. The less "like me" someone is, the greater my perceived risk of working with him or her. I may unconsciously believe that he or she will fail.

d. Be aware of the Pygmalion or Halo effect. Our beliefs about a person's potential for success or failure heavily influence the outcome. When we believe people will be successful, they will; conversely, if we believe they will fail, it is very likely they will. (See the story of Robert at Plaxon in chapter six.)

"We've been working on diversity for two years and instead of having more satisfied employees, we've got more complaints. No one's happy with what we're doing. What I really need is some help so I can do what I'm paid to do. I don't need more training."

a. Understand what stage the organization is in. Anger, confusion and concern are natural in Stage One.

b. Ensure that everyone understands why the diversity and inclusion journey is essential to the success of the organization. When the roads get bumpy, knowing that there's ice cream and gelato at the next rest stop makes it easier to continue.

"What kind of place is this becoming? No more jokes, no 'offensive' posters, which means anything fun or funny, our e-mail is being looked at and you have to watch every word you say or you'll offend someone and end up getting fired. We had a four-hour training session about a year and a half ago, and it didn't do any good. People left there feeling like they were better off never saying anything to anyone."

a. Reiterate the business case for inclusivity.

b. Ensure that diversity and inclusivity are talked about at every opportunity. Emphasize the connection between a comfortable environment and productivity.

c. Remind employees that what one person thinks is humorous can seriously damage relationships with teammates and/or customers.

"People bring a lot of differences to the workplace that belong out-side. I don't talk about who I sleep with and don't want to know what anyone else is doing. Religion has no place in the workplace either. I don't understand why we have to let people leave early so they can practice their religion. I do mine on my day off."

a. Employees need to develop their multicultural competency. Education (not just training) should focus on moving from denial to acceptance.

b. The more employees understand about privilege – the in-visible knapsack — the easier it is for them to understand another person's perspective. When I understand that most businesses in the U.S. are closed on my Sabbath, Sunday, it's easier to let others have time off to celebrate their relig-ion.

The new employee has been told by several of his colleagues, "Everyone knows why you were hired." He asks for answers. "I don't want anyone to think that the reason I got this job is because I'm Cu-ban. I'm not a person of color or whatever is politically correct. I'm just a damned good engineer."

These statements require immediate action. The colleague's state-ment and the employee's response indicate that the environment is openly hostile and not inclusive.

a. Make sure to let the colleague who says "everyone knows why you were hired" know that she is walking on thin ice and may face disciplinary action if her actions are viewed as exclusive rather than inclusive.

b. Networks and affiliation groups are good places for mi-nority employees to see the value of diversity and to connect with others like themselves for comfort and sup-port. It is important for employees to know that their characteristics are important to the organization but not the reason for their hire.

c. Tie the organization's success to better utilizing the chang-ing demographics.

"I think this diversity stuff is a bunch of b-s. Everybody has the same chance to be successful here. If you fail it's because you're just not able to cut it. What should we do? Give someone extra credit because he's diverse? Well, when is it going to be my turn? Everybody has a day and a celebration but White men. All the time we're spending on these programs is costing us time and money."

a. Make sure the definition of diversity, in words, deeds, policies and practices, is inclusive – includes White men as well as others.
b. Talk about how diversity (in the broadest context) benefits the organization.
c. Make sure everyone knows what the organization expects from employees concerning supportive behaviors.
d. If you are using the Fairness business case be aware that people may have a different view of whether or not the organization is a meritocracy.

"Three of my colleagues have taken maternity leave in the past year, and two others are pregnant. Women who leave to have a baby never come back the same. Their commitment, work ethic, everything is different, and I have to pick up the extra work. Just because I don't have children, they think I don't deserve any time off. Last week I told my boss I had to leave early to take care of my imaginary baby. He laughed, but I said, 'Hey, it's the only way I get a break.'"

a. All of the actions and activities should indicate that the initiative is inclusive and supports all employees. When defining "balance" describe it in words and practices as "work and life" rather than "work and family" balance.
b. Conduct focus groups with single/no children employees to understand their issues and challenges.
c. Use the concept of "substitution" to answer the question of women and maternity leave. Few of us would be upset if someone who returned from medical leave for cancer treatment was not totally available while going through chemotherapy. Being a new parent is difficult, stressful and may require patience from co-workers.

"My manager doesn't have a clue about managing diversity. She says she supports it, and in the same breath she tells a joke making fun of one of the gay men in our group. Her boss thinks she's on board, so what can I do?"

a. Make sure employees know that when managers or peers say or do something that offends them they are expected to *do* something to address it. Suggest that at the first opportunity that "fits" the person and the organization, they let the person know what bothered them and how they would prefer the person to behave in the future.

b. People will live up to or down to our expectations. You could say to your manager, "I was surprised when I heard you making that joke. That is really out of character for you. I've always thought of you as a leader in this area." This lets her live *up* to your expectations.

c. If you are the leader and you hear this from employees (perhaps in a focus group session) use this "teachable moment" to illustrate for managers the importance of modeling the behaviors that support inclusivity and diversity. Let them know that people do what managers do and not what managers say.

"I think the most difficult issue we face is style differences. Race, gender and those things don't matter here, but if you're not an analytic, you'll never be successful."

a. Give the person positive feedback and help him/her understand how to talk about style diversity as an asset.

b. Do not ignore the significance of race and gender issues. Style or function may be crucial in the organization, but race and gender are two of the most prevalent and difficult characteristics to address.

"The leadership says it cares about diversity, and yet there aren't any Black or Hispanics in senior management. It's all lip service. We just came back from a great training session on Asian culture. Too bad none of the managers showed up. They are the ones who really need this training. Why don't they ever show up at any of these events? I've been here fifteen years, and nothing has changed. I'm not investing any time in this 'new' effort."

There are two distinct questions in this statement.

a. The first statement ("there aren't any Blacks...") is an indication that attention needs to be paid to ensuring that the definition of diversity is more than race. It is crucial that everyone know that "lip service" is more than "visible diversity."

b. Ask for suggestions on how the organization can change its Rolodex to increase the likelihood that it will become more visibly diverse. Measure employees on their contribution to recruiting visible diversity. (See the 7Keys Scorecard® in chapter seven.)

c. The second part (...none of the managers showed up.") must be addressed. Managers' measurements need to include visible leadership at company events. Managers are role models, whether they want to be or not. Their participation is seen as supporting the journey and the initiative's importance. Remember: "Example is not the main thing in influencing others. It is the only thing." (Albert Schweitzer)

d. Discuss the three stages, the organization's progress to date and what it will take to move forward on the journey.

"We're all really just human beings. Why can't we all be treated the same, live by the same rules and forget about all these differences?"

   a. On the continuum of cultural competency, this is the stage of cultural blindness. Help employees understand the negatives of this stage and how to move along the continuum.
   b. Talk about how diversity (in the broadest context) benefits the organization and how ignoring diversity negatively impact progress.

Appendix B

Sample Scorecard *Questions*

Section 1: Clearly Articulate & Communicate Vision and Strategy

1. Do you have an organization-specific diversity or inclusivity plan?
2. Do you have a strategy for communicating the organization's diversity plan?
3. In the past 12 months how many diversity-related (business- or organization-specific) communications activities have you completed? Examples: Distributed "The Diversity Vision" or shared reports related to your diversity strategy plans, goals or progress?

Section 2: Diversifying the Candidate Pool

1. In the last 12 months how many diversity or inclusion activities (e.g., career fairs or job fairs) have you participated in?
2. In the past 12 months how many exploratory interviews have you conducted?
3. In the past 12 months how many exploratory interviews have your direct reports conducted?

Section 3: Increasing Inclusivity

1. Do you have established flex policies in place (e.g., flex time, telecommuting, paternity leave)?
2. Do your employees feel comfortable using these policies and practices?

Section 4: Developing Leadership Skills

1. In the last 12 months how many personal development activities have you done (e.g., read articles, initiated conversations, attended events)?

2. Are you a member of any organization where you are in the "minority"? If so, how many?
3. Do your employees view you as a leader and champion of diversity?

Level Two Manager Scorecard *Sample Questions*

Section 1: Clearly Articulate and Communicate Vision and Strategy

1. Do you have an organization-specific diversity or inclusivity plan?
2. Do you have a strategy for communicating the organization's diversity and inclusivity plan?
3. In the past 12 months how many diversity-related business or organization-specific communications activities have you completed? Examples: Distributed the diversity vision or shared reports related to your inclusivity strategy plans, goals or progress?

Section 2: Coach, Mentor and Sponsor

1. What is your level of participation in company or group-sponsored mentoring, "buddy" or coaching activities?
2. At what level are your direct reports involved in programs to mentor, coach or sponsor others?
3. Are you a mentor, coach or sponsor for any employee(s) in the organization?
4. Are you a mentor, coach or sponsor for anyone outside the organization?

Section 3: Support Diversity Teams

1. Does your business/group have an established and functioning diversity council or team?
2. In the past 12 months how many times have you shared what the company or your organization's diversity team is doing with your staff?

3. Do you have an established and functioning reward system for employees who further the diversity and inclusivity effort, e.g., Executive Diversity & Inclusivity Council members?

Level Three Individual Contributor Scorecard
Sample Questions

Section 1: Clearly Articulate and Communicate Vision and Strategy

1. Have you actively sought information about your organization's inclusivity vision and/or plan?
2. Have you sought information about your business/group's diversity team?
3. In the past 12 months how many times have you discussed or shared what your organization's diversity team is doing with peers or colleagues?
4. Have you volunteered to actively assist the diversity effort, e.g., as a member of the diversity team/council?
5. In the past 12 months how many diversity-related conversations or discussions have you initiated?

Section 2: Career Development and Mentoring

1. Have you participated in any group or organization's mentoring or "buddy" activity?
2. Are you a mentor, buddy, coach or sponsor for any employee(s)?
3. Does your career development plan include specific diversity-related strategies or actions?

Section 3: Making the Candidate Pool More Diverse

1. In the last 12 months how many diversity outreach activities (e.g., career fairs and conferences) have you volunteered for or participated in?
2. In the past 12 months how many times have you consciously acted to help the diversity recruiting effort?

Appendix C

Further Reading

Adams, Maurianne (Ed) et al. *Readings for Diversity and Social Justice: An Anthology on Racism, Sexism, Anti-Semitism, Heterosexism, Classism, and Ableism.* Philadelphia: Falmer Press, 2000.

Bennett, M. J. (Ed.). *Basic Concepts of Intercultural Communication.* Selected readings. Yarmouth, ME: Intercultural Press, 1998.

Blanchard, Ken. *Peacock in the Land of Penguins.* San Francisco: Berrett-Koehler Publishers, 2001.

Caver, Keith, and Livers, Ancella. "Dear White Boss..." Harvard Business Review Nov 2002.

Cox, Taylor. *Creating the Multicultural Organization: A Strategy for Capturing the Power of Diversity* San Francisco: Berrett-Koehler 2002.

Esty, Katharine, Griffin, Richard, and Hirsch, Marcie Schorr. *Workplace Diversity: A Manager's Guide to Solving Problems and Turning Diversity into a Competitive Advantage.* Holbrook MA: Adams Media Corporation, 1995.

Hayashi, Alden M. "Mommy-Track Backlash." Harvard Business Review 2001.

Hitchcock, Jeff and Crandall, Dostie *Lifting the White Veil: An Exploration of White American Culture in a Multiracial Context.* Roselle NJ: Crandall Dostie & Douglass Books, 2002.

Johnson, Allan G. *Privilege, Power, and Difference,* New York: McGraw-Hill 2001.

Katz, Judith, *White Awareness: Handbook for Anti-Racism Training.* University of Oklahoma Press, 2003.

Loden Marilyn. *Implementing Diversity*, New York: McGraw-Hill 1995.

Mayer, J. D., & Salovey, P. *Emotional Intelligence and the Construction and Regulation of Feelings.* Applied and Preventive Psychology, (1995) 197-208.

Mayer, J. D., & Salovey, P. *The Intelligence of Emotional Intelligence.* Intelligence, 17(4), (1993) 433-442.

Meyerson, Debra and Fletcher, Joyce K. "A Modest Manifesto for Shattering the Glass Ceiling." *Harvard Business Review* January/February, 2000.

Miller, Fredrick A, and Katz, Judith H. *The Inclusion Breakthrough.* San Francisco: Berrett-Koehler, 2002

Morrison, Ann M. *The New Leader: Guidelines on Leadership Diversity in America.* San Francisco: Jossey-Bass Publishers, 1992.

Rothenbert, Paula S. *White Privilege : Essential Readings on the Other Side of Racism.* New York: Worth Publishers, 2001.

Salovey, P., & Sluyter, D. J. *Emotional Development and Emotional Intelligence.* New York: Basic Books 1997.

Schrank, Robert. "Two Women, Three Men on a Raft." Harvard Business Review, 1994.

Sonnenschein, William. *Diversity Toolkit: How You Can Build and Benefit from a Diverse Workforce.* New York: McGraw-Hill 1999.

Thomas, David A. "Diversity As Strategy." Harvard Business Review September 2004.

Thomas, David A. and Ely, Robin J. "Making Differences Matter: A New Paradigm for Managing Diversity." Harvard Business Review 2001.

Trompenaars, Fons, and Hampden-Turner, Charles. *Riding the Waves of Culture.* New York: McGraw Hill, 1998.

Williams Mark A., *The 10 Lenses: Your Guide to Living & Working in a Multicultural World.* VA: Capital Books, 2001.

Williamson, Alistair D. "Is This the Right Time to Come Out?" Harvard Business Review 2001

West, Cornel. *Race Matters.* New York: Vintage: 1994.

Endnotes

i Encarta® World English Dictionary © 1999 Microsoft Corporation. All rights reserved. Developed for Microsoft by Bloomsbury Publishing.

ii Steven Covey, Seven Habits of Highly Effective People: Powerful Lessons in Personal Change Press; 1st edition (September 15, 1990).

iii Encarta® World English Dictionary © 1999 Microsoft Corporation. All rights reserved. Developed for Microsoft by Bloomsbury Publishing Plc.

iv W.C. Howell and E.A. Fleishman (cds.), Human Performance and Productivity. Vol 2: Information Processing and Decision Making. Hillsdale, NJ: Erlbaum; 1982. (Thanks A Trost).

v Encarta® World English Dictionary © 1999 Microsoft Corporation. All rights reserved. Developed for Microsoft by Bloomsbury Publishing Plc.

vi Ibid

vii Peggy McIntosh, White Privilege and Male Privilege, Wellesley Center for Research on Women, 1988.

viii Encarta® World English Dictionary © 1999 Microsoft Corporation. All rights reserved. Developed for Microsoft by Bloomsbury Publishing Plc.

ix The 'company name' is entirely fictional - any similarity to any real company is purely coincidental.

x Ibid

xi Four Famous Embroidery Styles, China Window.com, Google®.

xii 2003 Functional Diversity Primer (2003) Diversity Best Practices, 1990 M Street, NW, Washington, D.C., 20036.

xiii Ibid

xiv U.S. Department of Labor, Office of Federal Contract Compliance Programs Executive Order 11246 of 1965.

xv Ely, Robin J., and Thomas, David A., Cultural Diversity at Work: The Effects of Diversity Perspectives on Work Group Processes and Outcomes, Administrative Science Quarterly. June 2001; Vol. 46, Issue.

xvi R. Roosevelt Thomas, From Affirmative Action to Affirming Diversity, Harvard Business Review 1989.

xvii The 'company name' is entirely fictional - any similarity to any real company is purely coincidental.

xviii Ibid

xix Salovey, P. & Mayer, J.D. (1990). Emotional Intelligence. Imagination, Cognition, and Personality, 9, 185-211.

xx Ibid

xxi Hot buttons are emotional triggers set off by what people do and say to others.

xxii Opportunities that enlighten, illustrate a concept like empathy or provide a lesson.

xxiii Peggy McIntosh White Privilege and Male Privilege, Wellesley Center for Research on Women, 1988

xxiv National Association for the Advancement of Colored People, One of the oldest civil rights organizations in America.

xxv Daniel Aronson, Overview of Systems Thinking© 1996-8.

xxvi R. Roosevelt Thomas, From Affirmative Action to Affirming Diversity, Harvard Business Review 1989.

xxvii R. Roosevelt Thomas Jr., Beyond Race and Gender, American Management Association, New York, 1991.

xxviii Encarta® World English Dictionary © 1999 Microsoft Corporation. All rights reserved. Developed for Microsoft by Bloomsbury Publishing

xxix Creating Cultural Competence University of San Diego, Irvine Grant II.

xxx Milton J. Bennett, Towards a Developmental Model of Intercultural Sensitivity. Michael Paige (editor), Education for the Intercultural Experience. Yormouth, Maine: Intercultural Press, 1993.

xxxi Mason, J. L., Cross, T., Rider, M. & Friesen, B. (1998). Developing cultural competence for agencies. Focal Point, 2 (4), 5-7.

xxxii James M. Patton and Norma Day-Vines, A Curriculum and Pedagogy for Cultural Competence: Strategies to Guide the Training of Special and General Education Teachers, The College of William and Mary, June 2001.

xxxiii Ibid

xxxiv Edward. E Hubbard, Measuring Diversity Results, Volume 1, Global Insights Publishing, 1977.

xxxv David Cottrell, Monday Morning Leadership, CornerStone Leadership Institute, 2002.

xxxvi R. Roosevelt Thomas, Building a House for Diversity, AMA Publications, 1999.

xxxvii Kent M. Keith, Anyway: The Paradoxical Commandments: Finding Personal Meaning in a Crazy World

Index

V

W

Z